The New Generation of
MANGA ARTISTS

THE Renga PORTFOLIO

Vol. 3

THE NEW GENERATAION OF MANGA ARTISTS
VOL. 3: The Renga Portfolio
by Renga

Copyright © 2003 Renga
Copyright © 2003 Graphic-sha Publishing Co., Ltd

This book was first designed and published in Japan in 2003 by Graphic-sha Publishing Co., Ltd.
This English edition was published in 2003 by Graphic-sha Publishing Co., Ltd.
Sansou Kudan Bldg. 4th Floor, 1-14-17 Kudan-kita, Chiyoda-ku, Tokyo 102-0073 Japan
Tel: +81-(0)3-3263-4318 Fax: +81-(0)3-3263-4318

Original Cover and Text Page Design: Shinichi Ishioka
English translation management: Língua fránca, Inc. (an3y-skmt@asahi-net.or.jp)
Editor: Kuniyoshi Masujima (Graphic-sha Publishing Co., Ltd.)
Foreign Language edn. Project Coordinator: Kumiko Sakamoto (Graphic-sha Publishing Co., Ltd.)

First printing: May 2003
Second printing: June 2003

ISBN: 4-7661-1365-9
Printed and bound in China by Everbest Printing Co., Ltd.

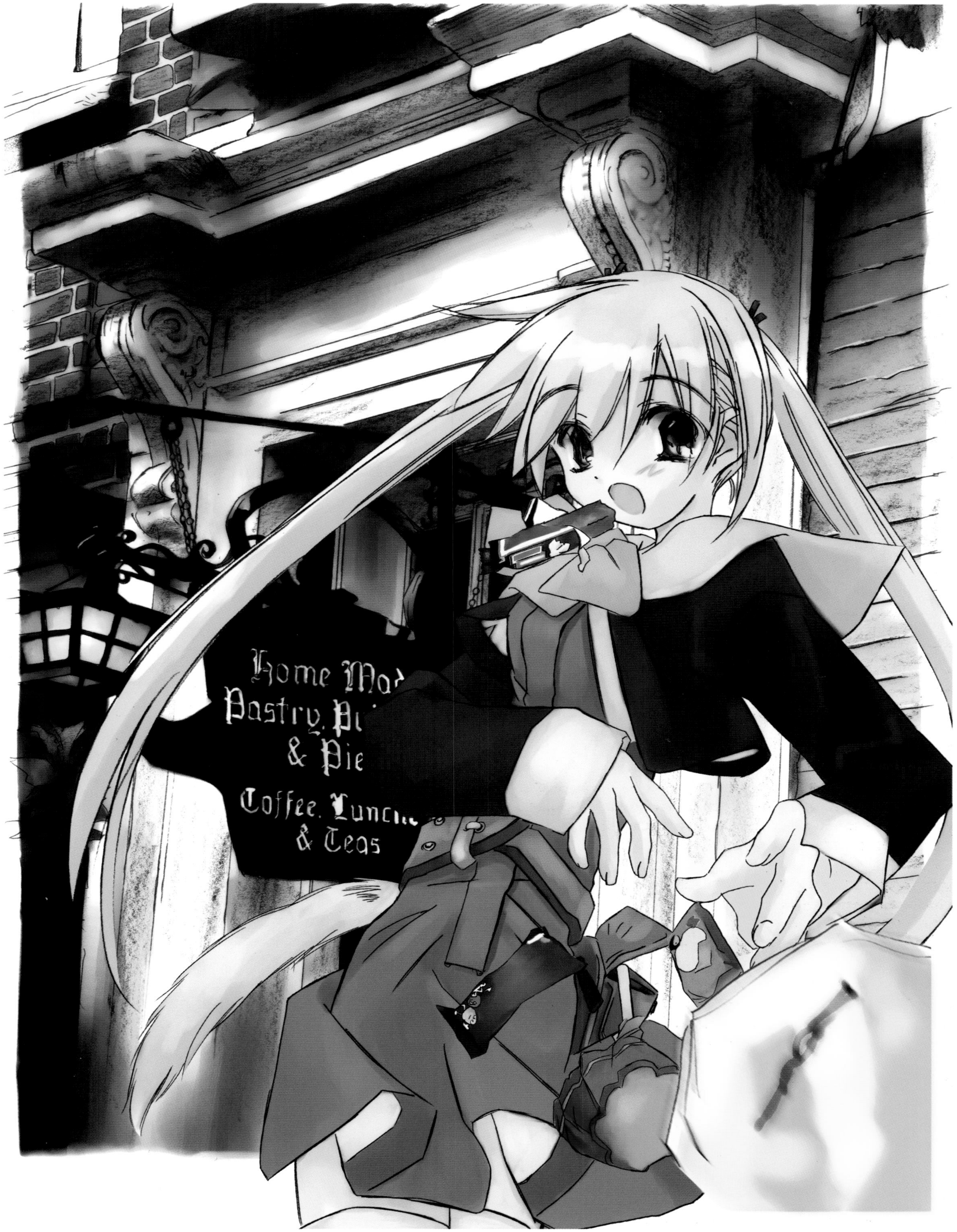
Home
Pastry,
Coffee,
& Teas

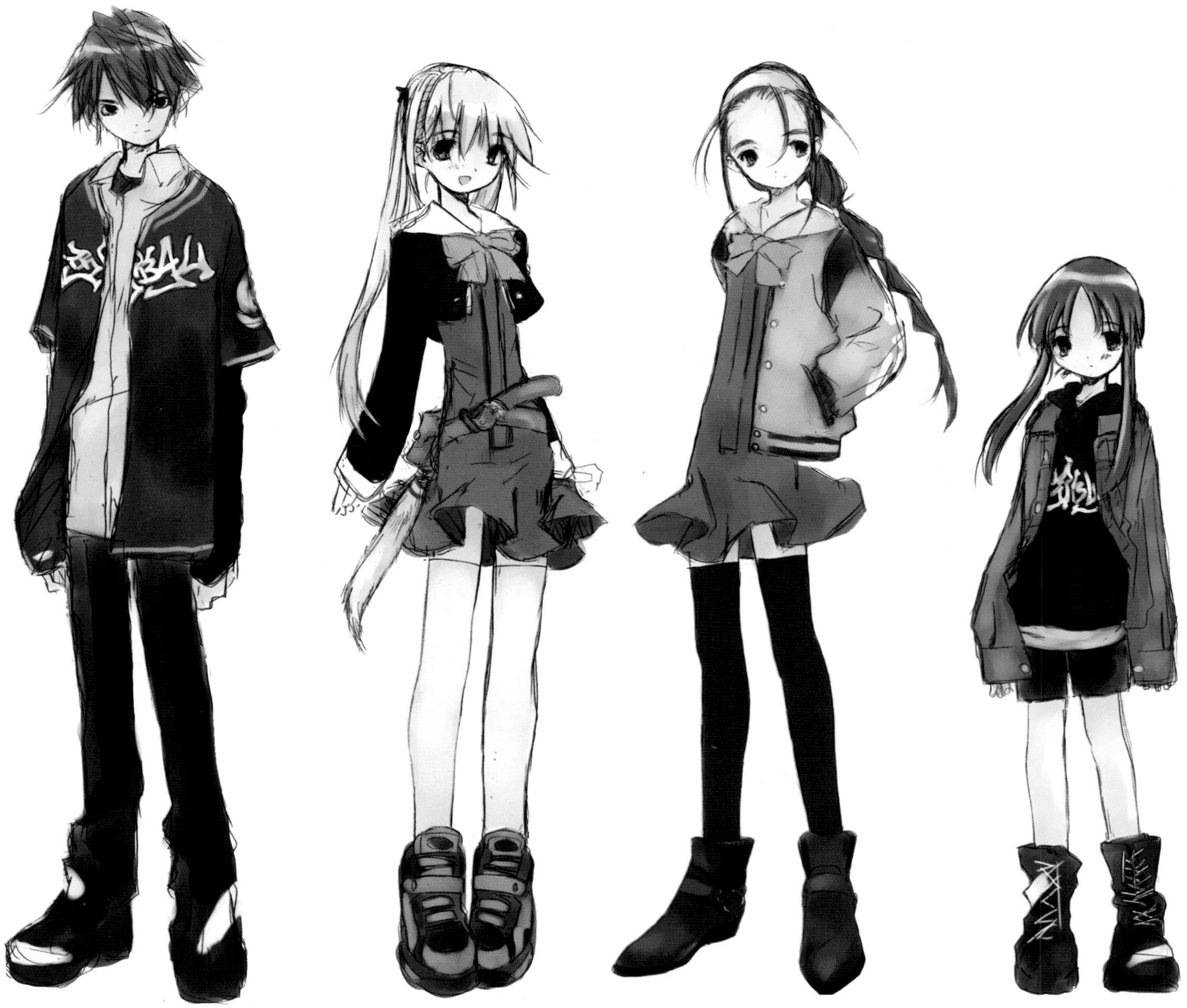

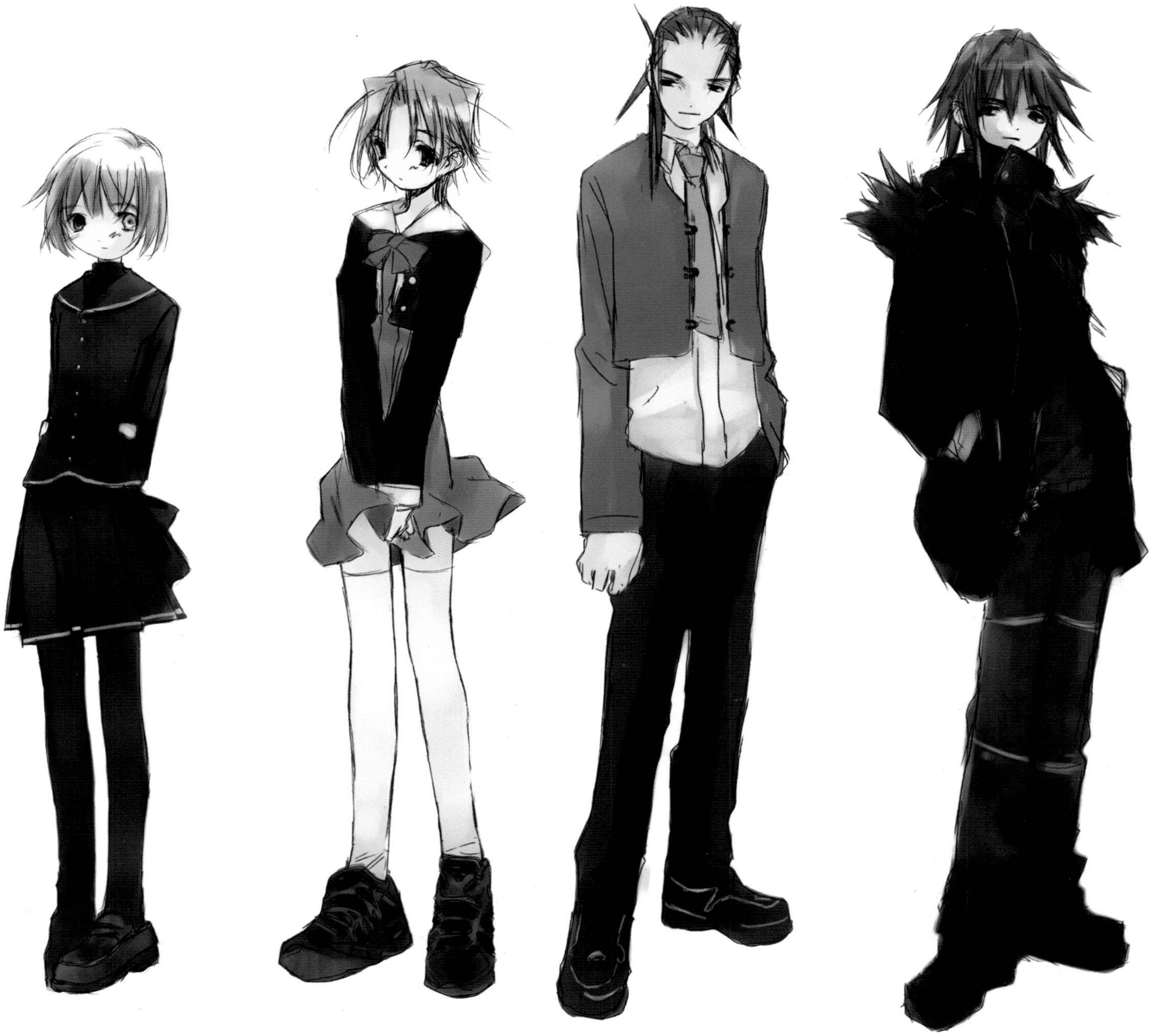

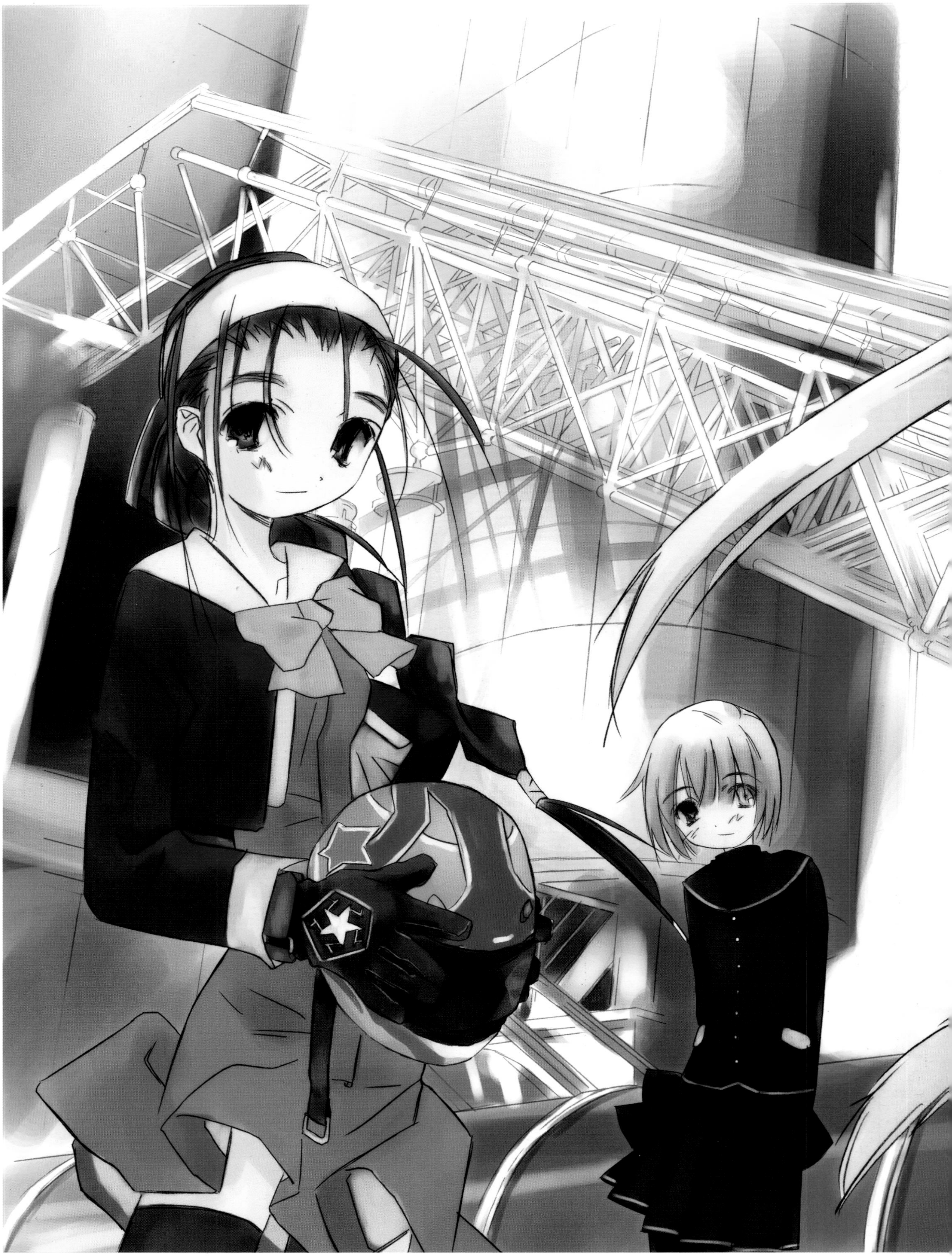

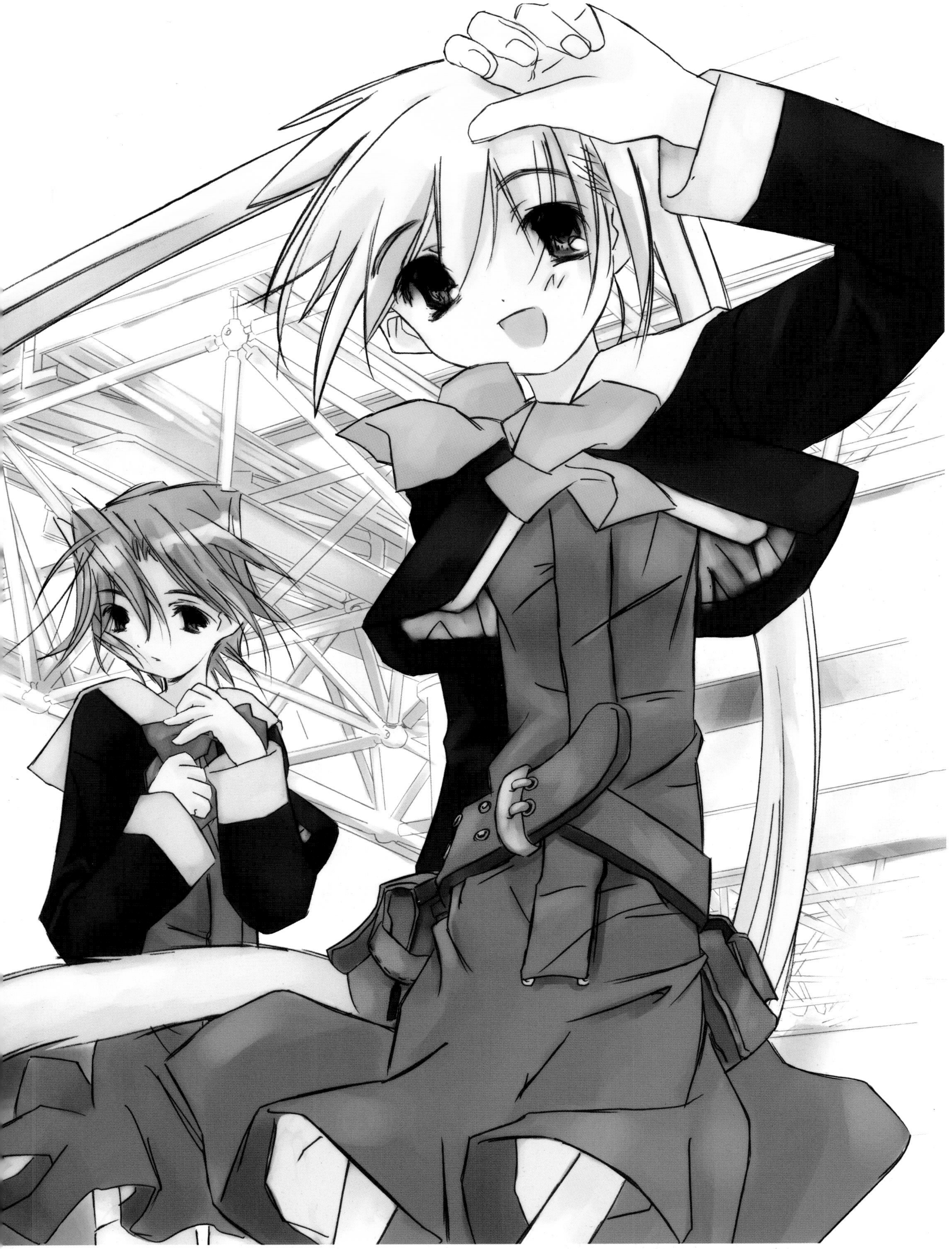

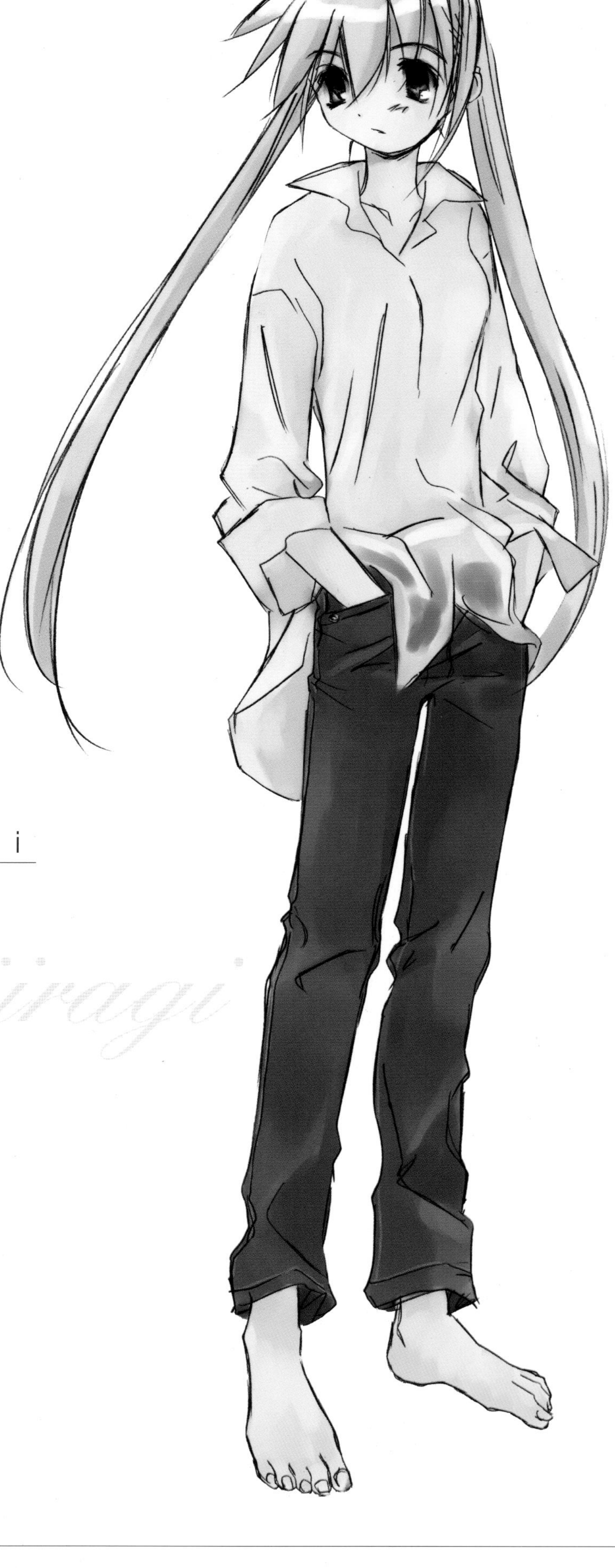

■ Oriha Hiiragi

Oriha Hiiragi

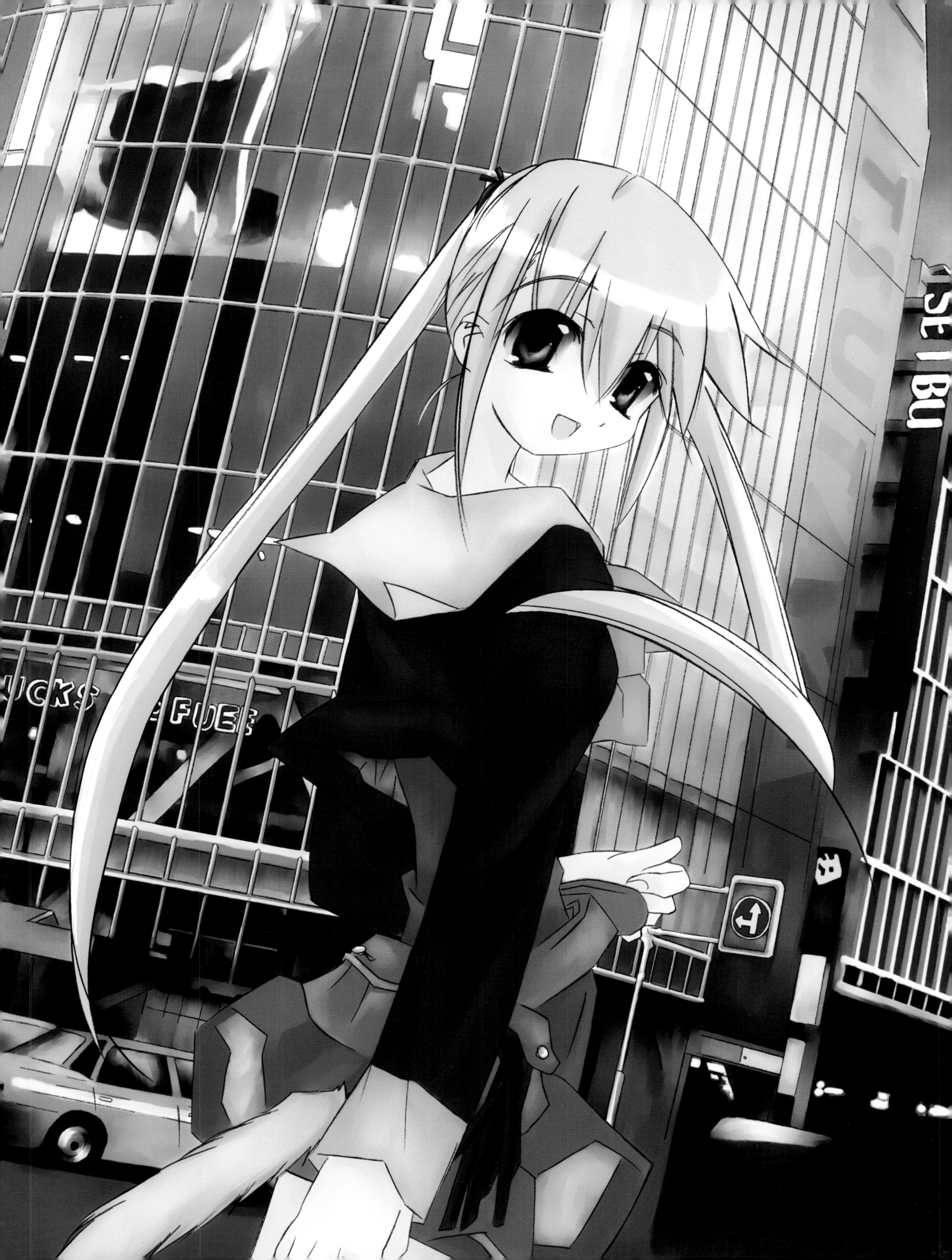

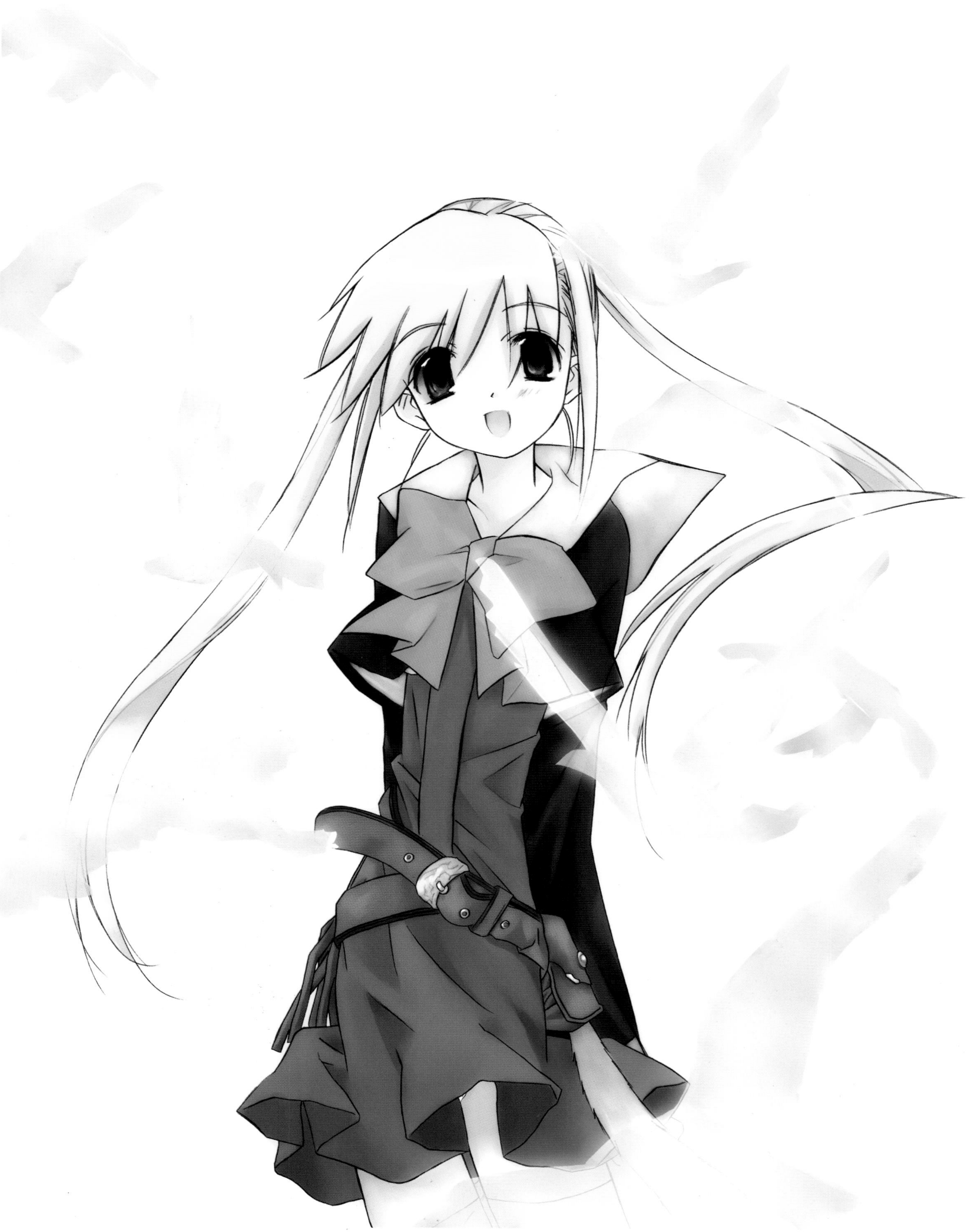

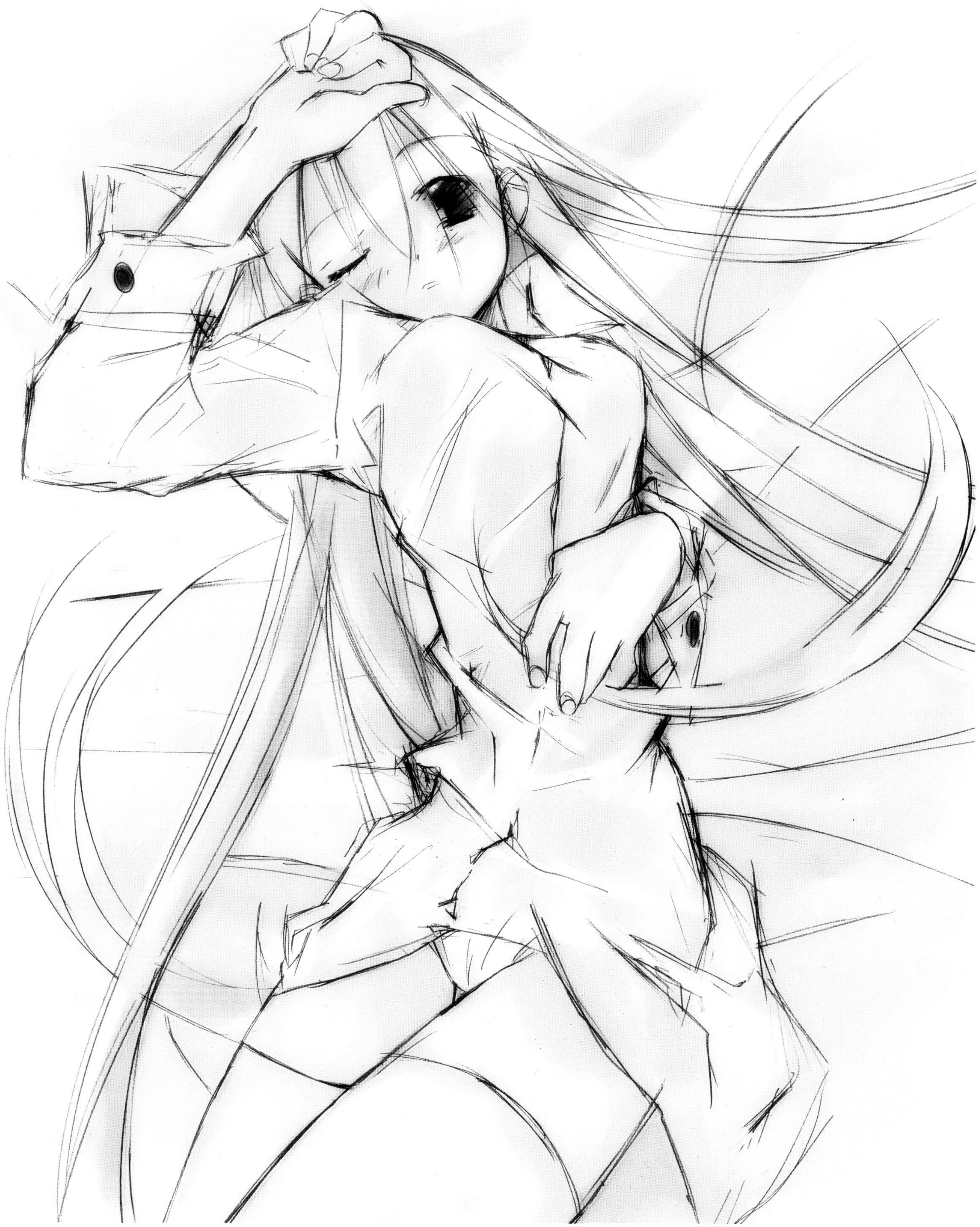

K a y a   k u n a m i ■

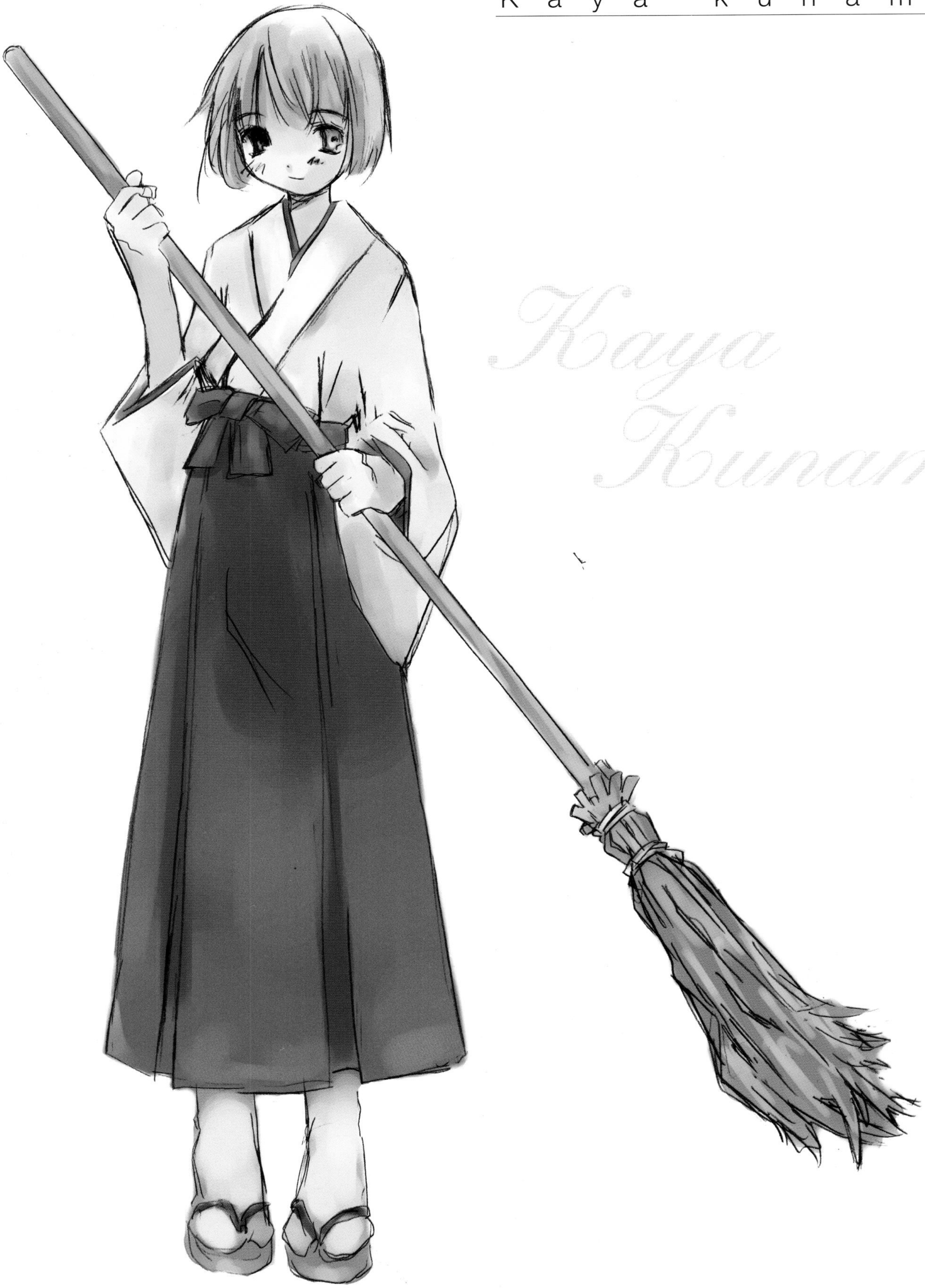

Kaya Kunami

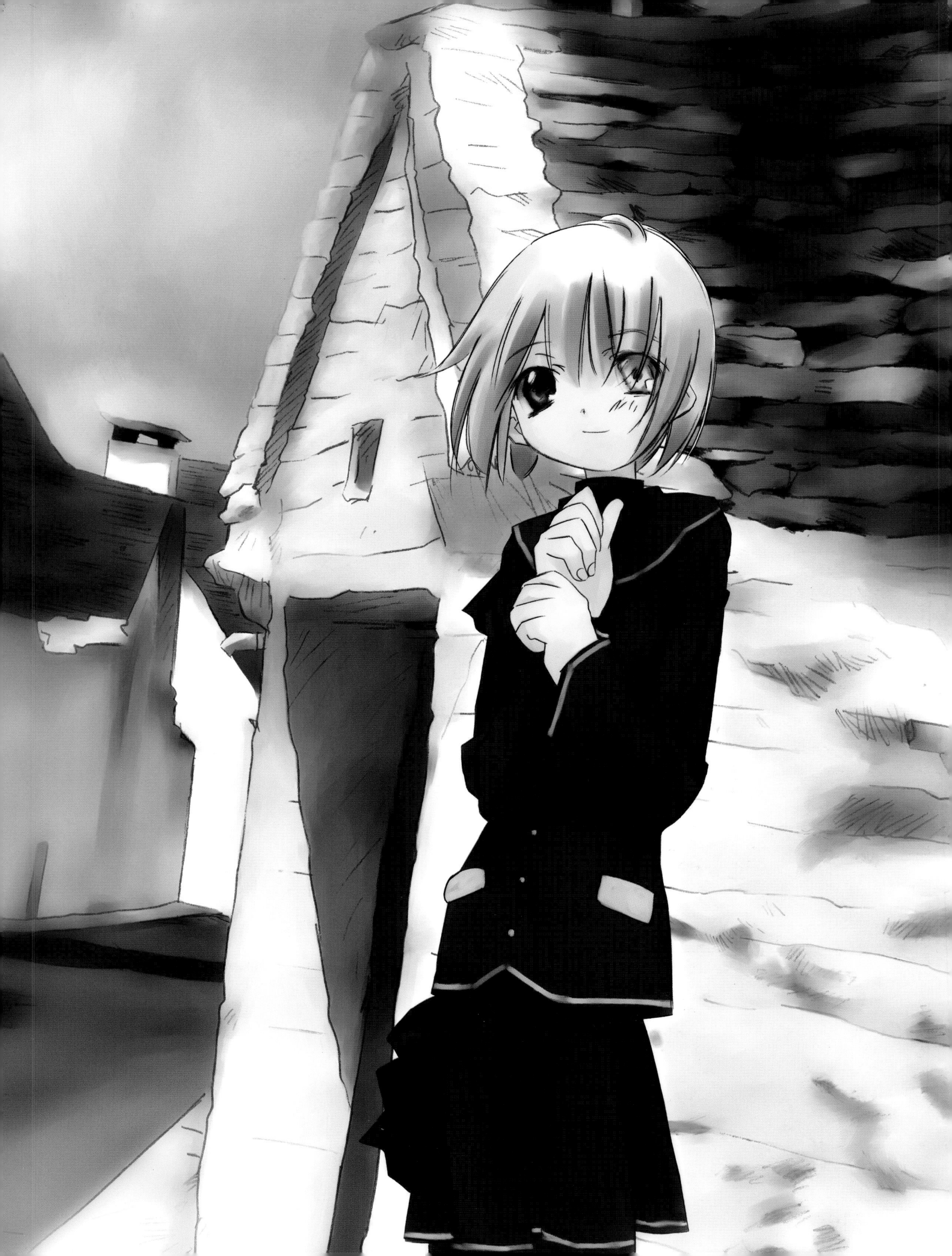

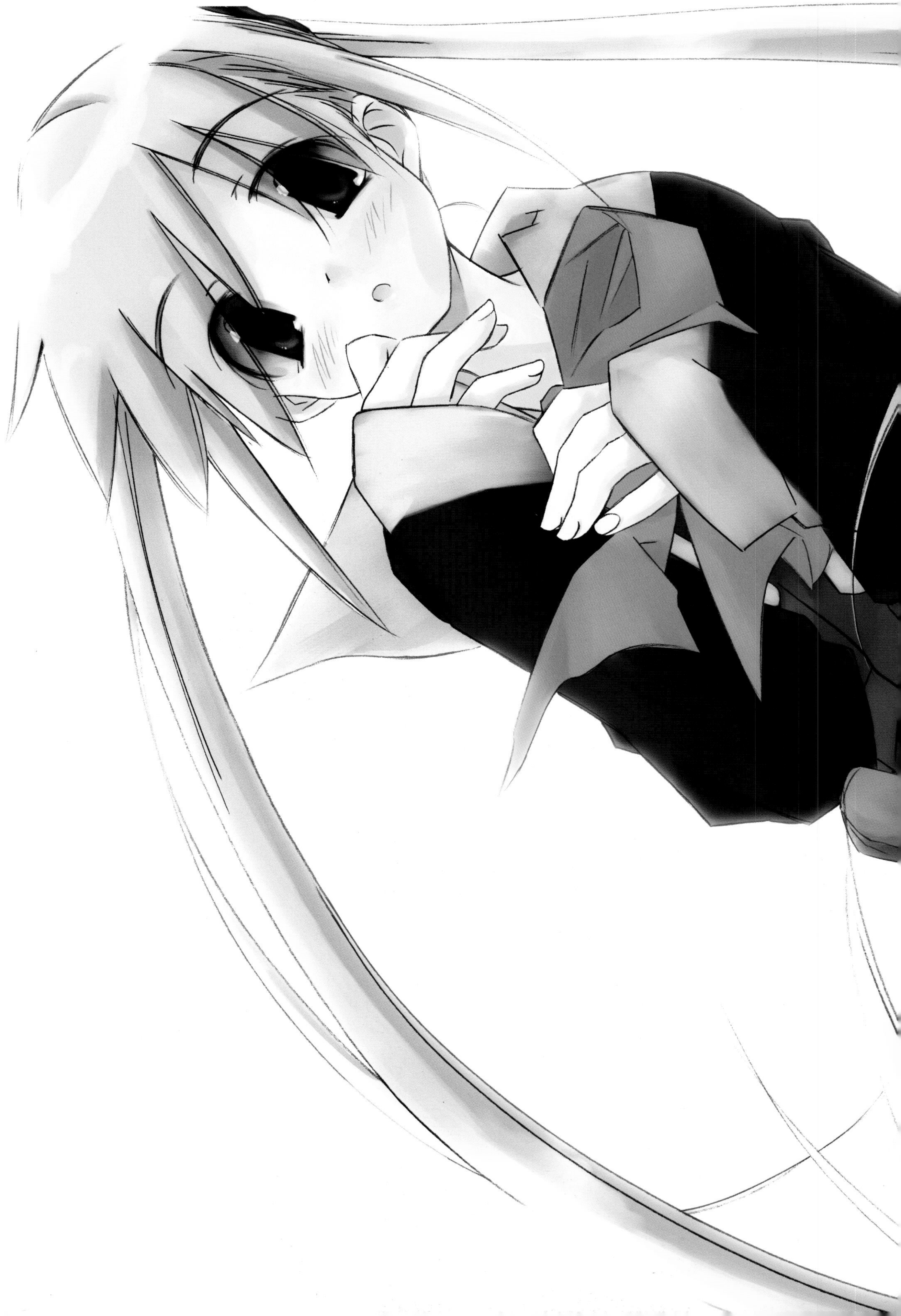

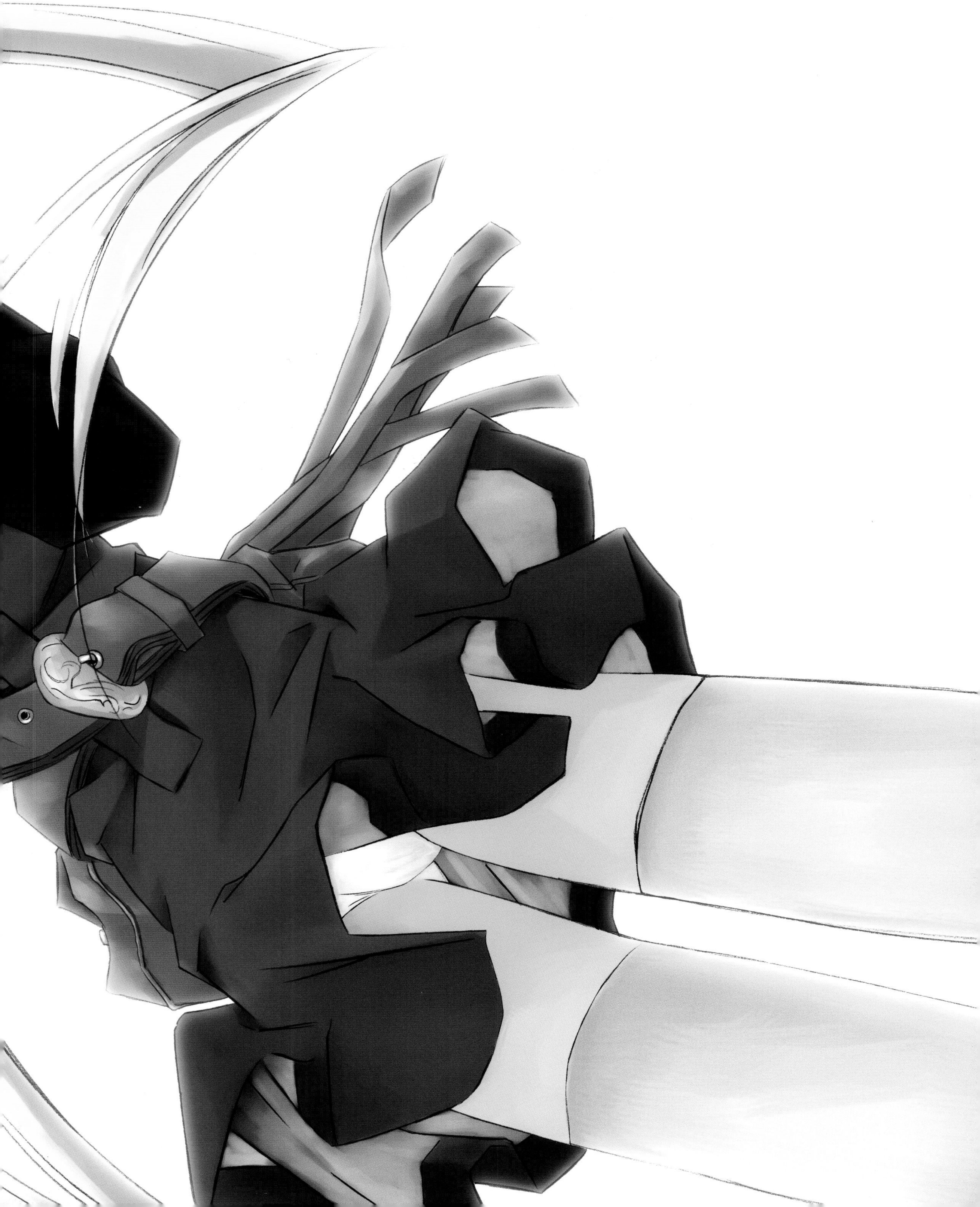

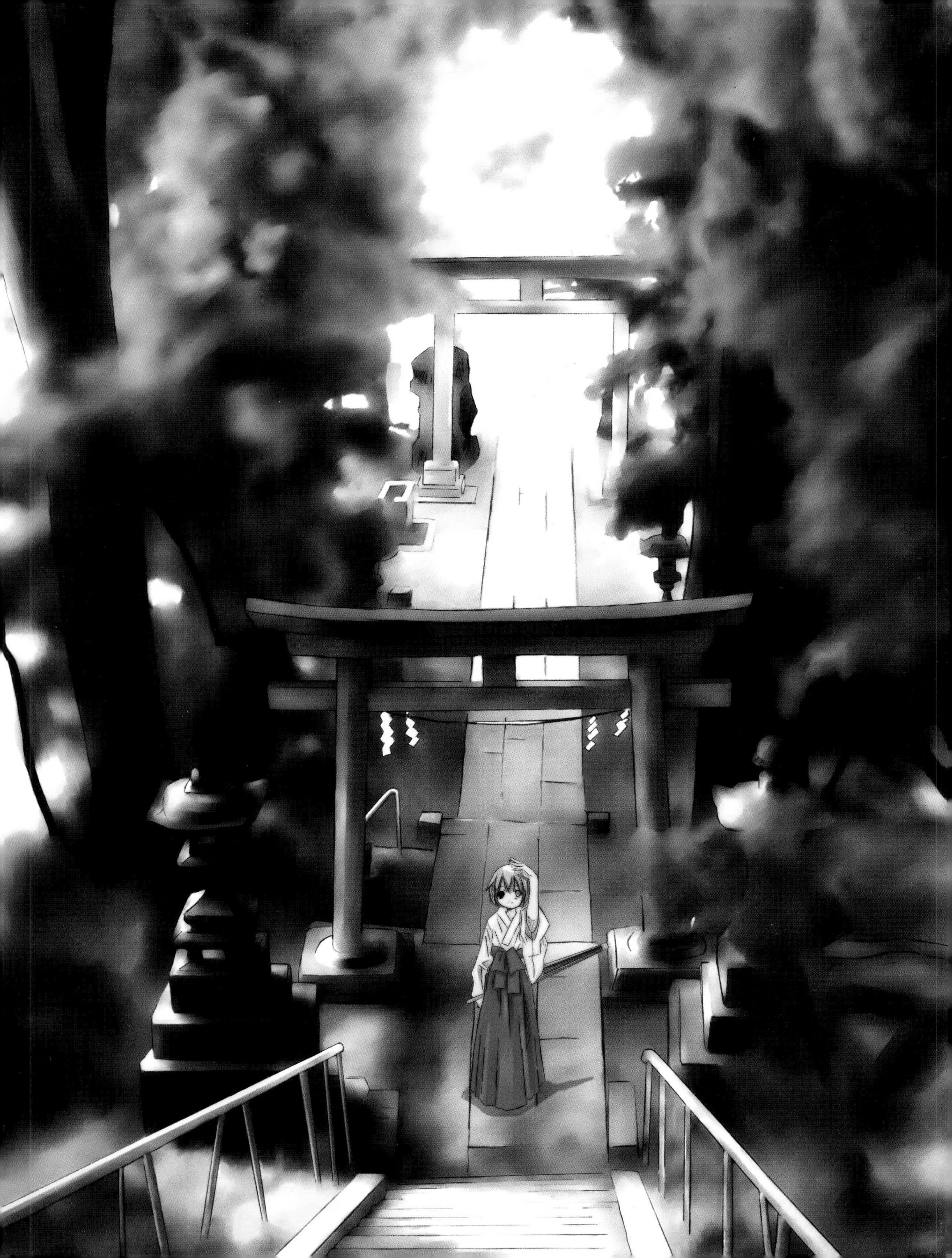

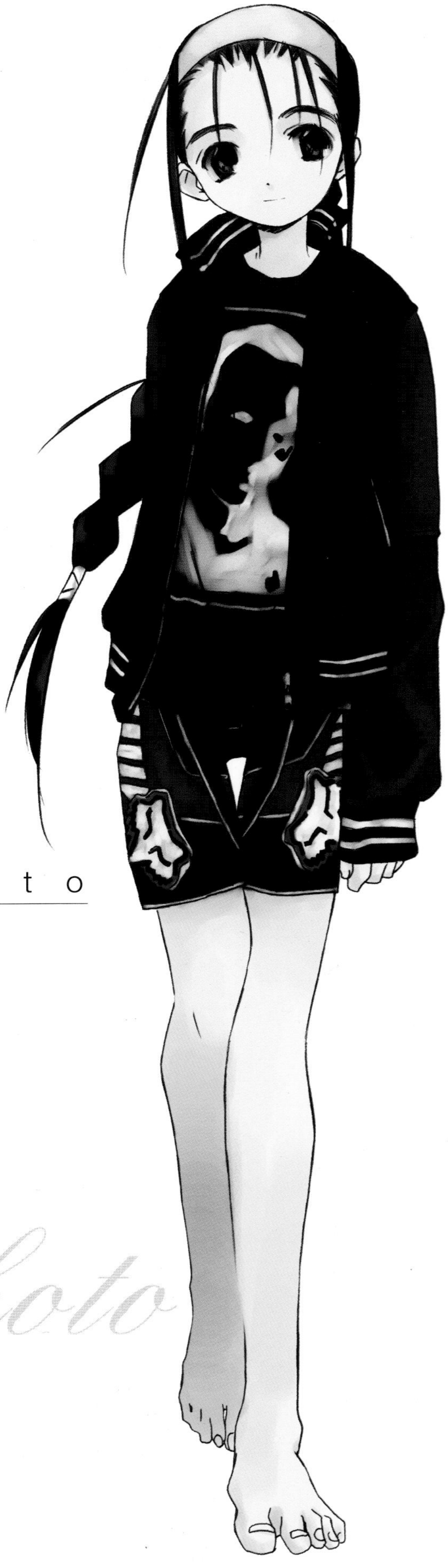

■ A k a n e H a s h i m o t o

Akane Hashoto

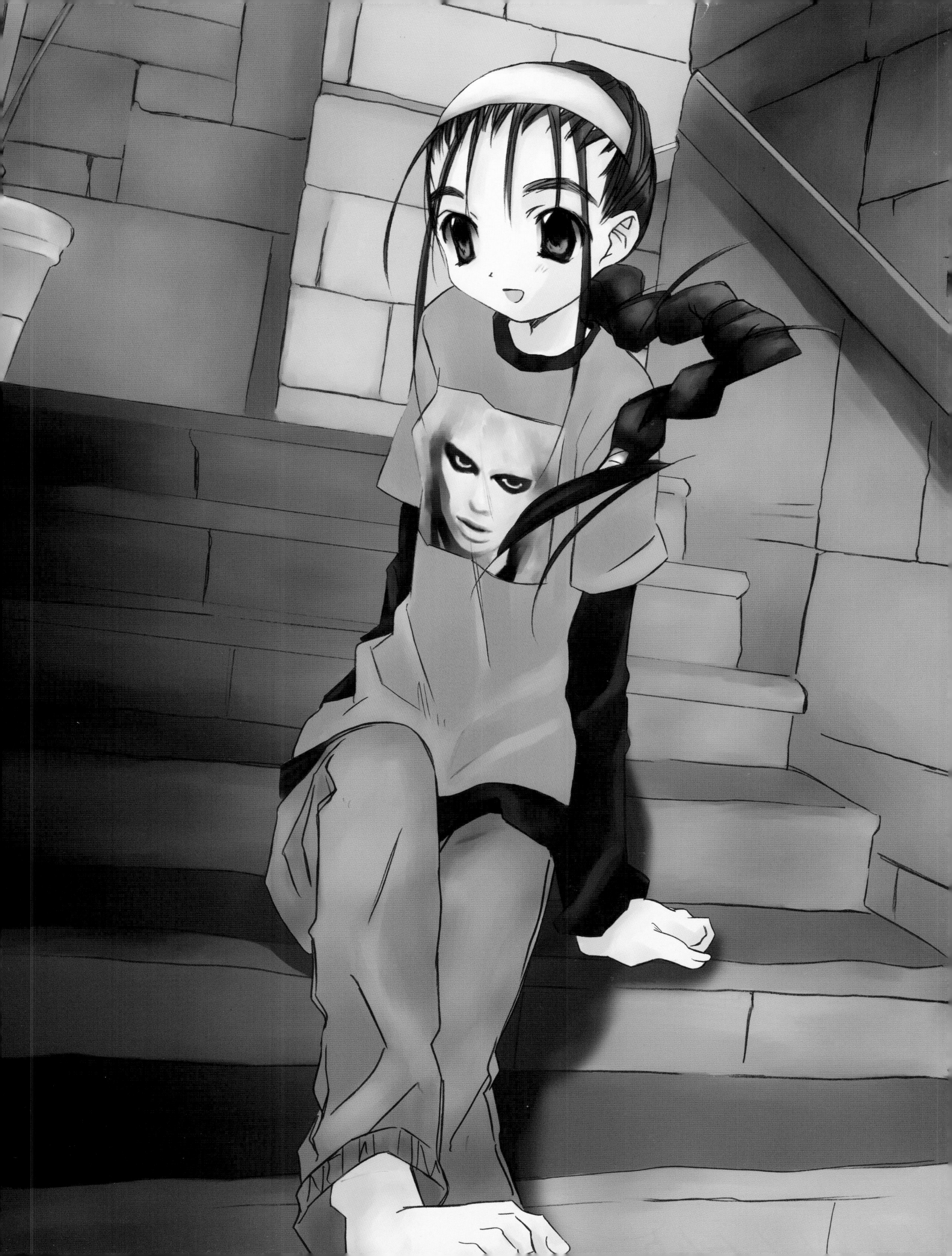

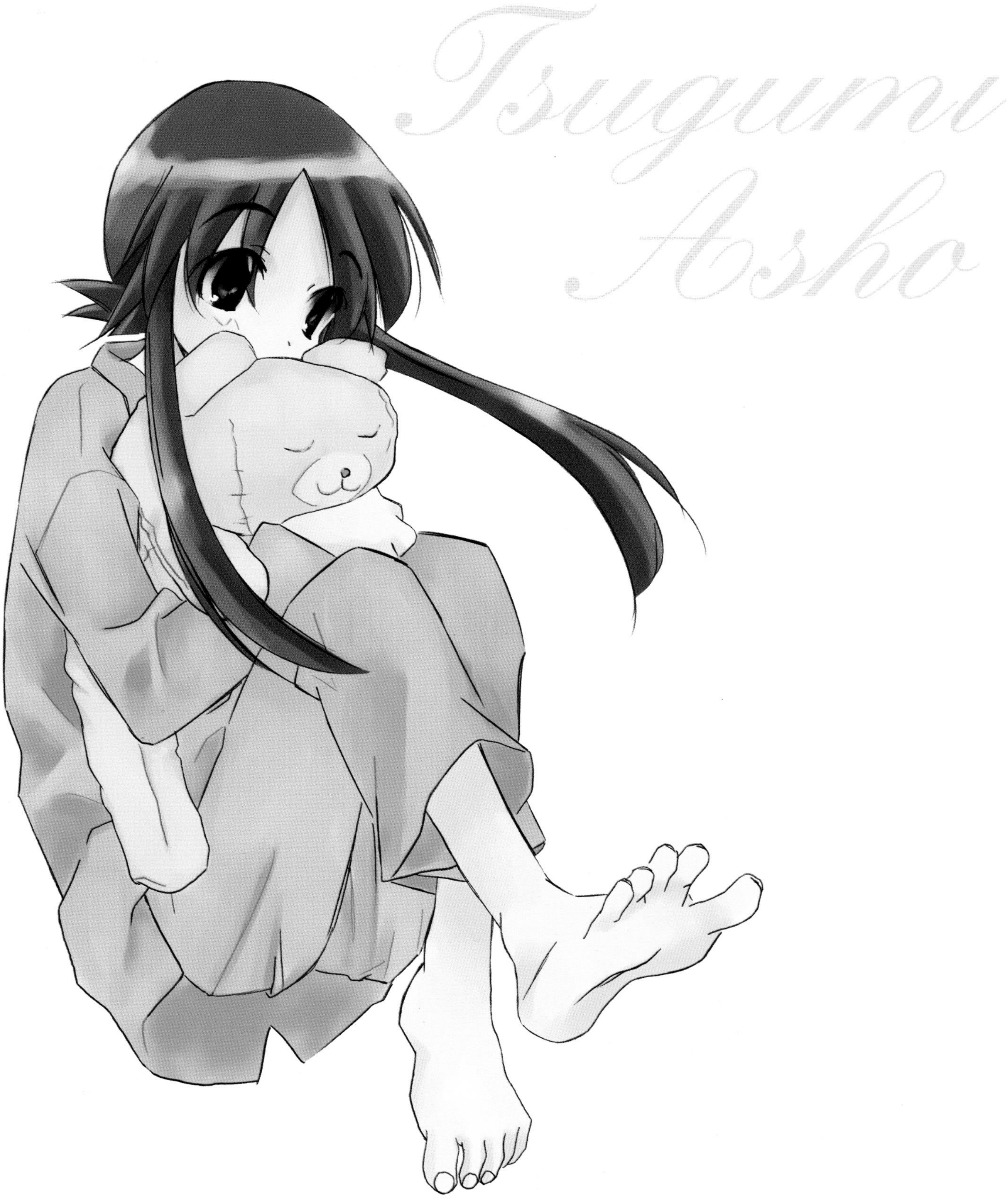
Tsugumi
Asho

Tsugumi Asho

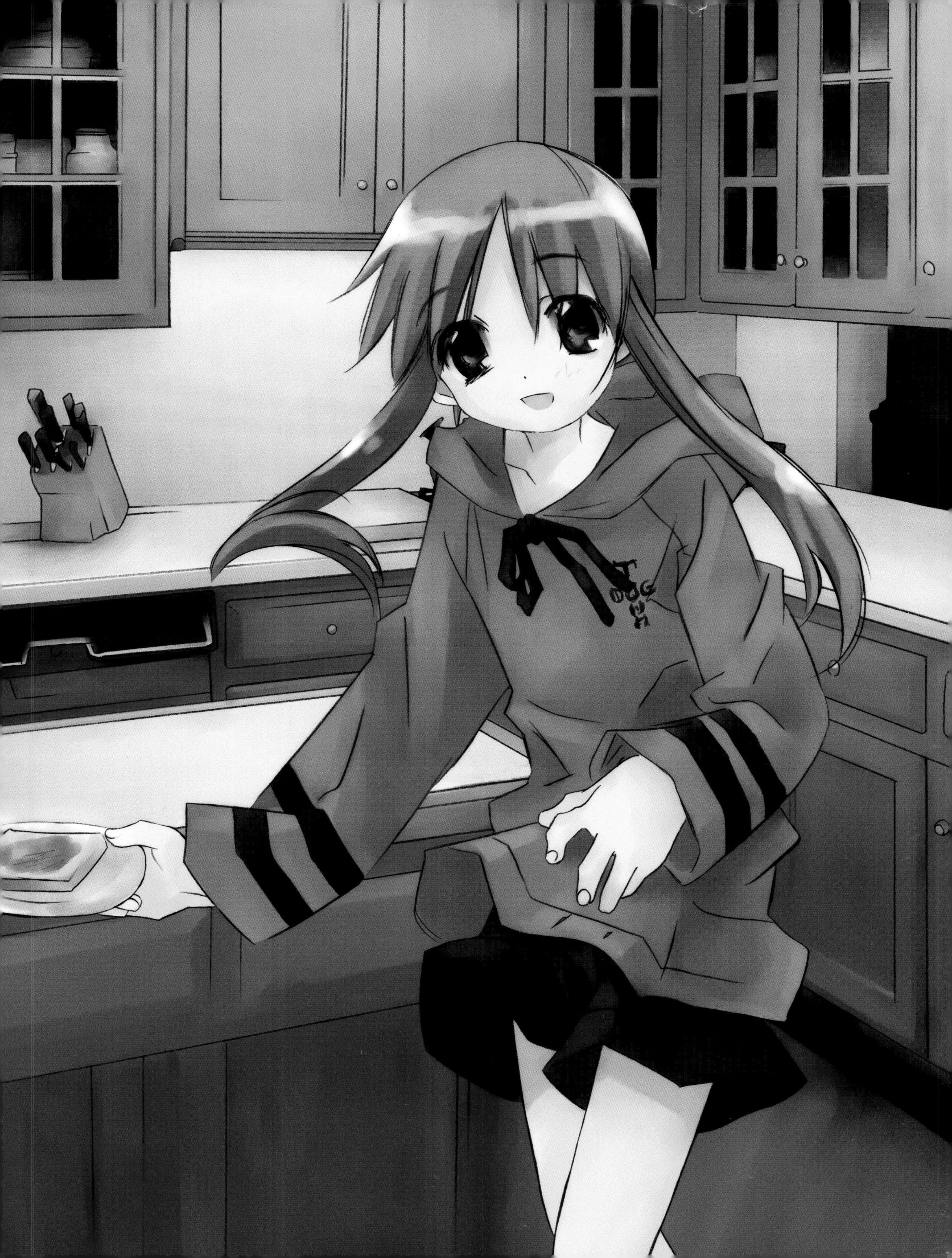

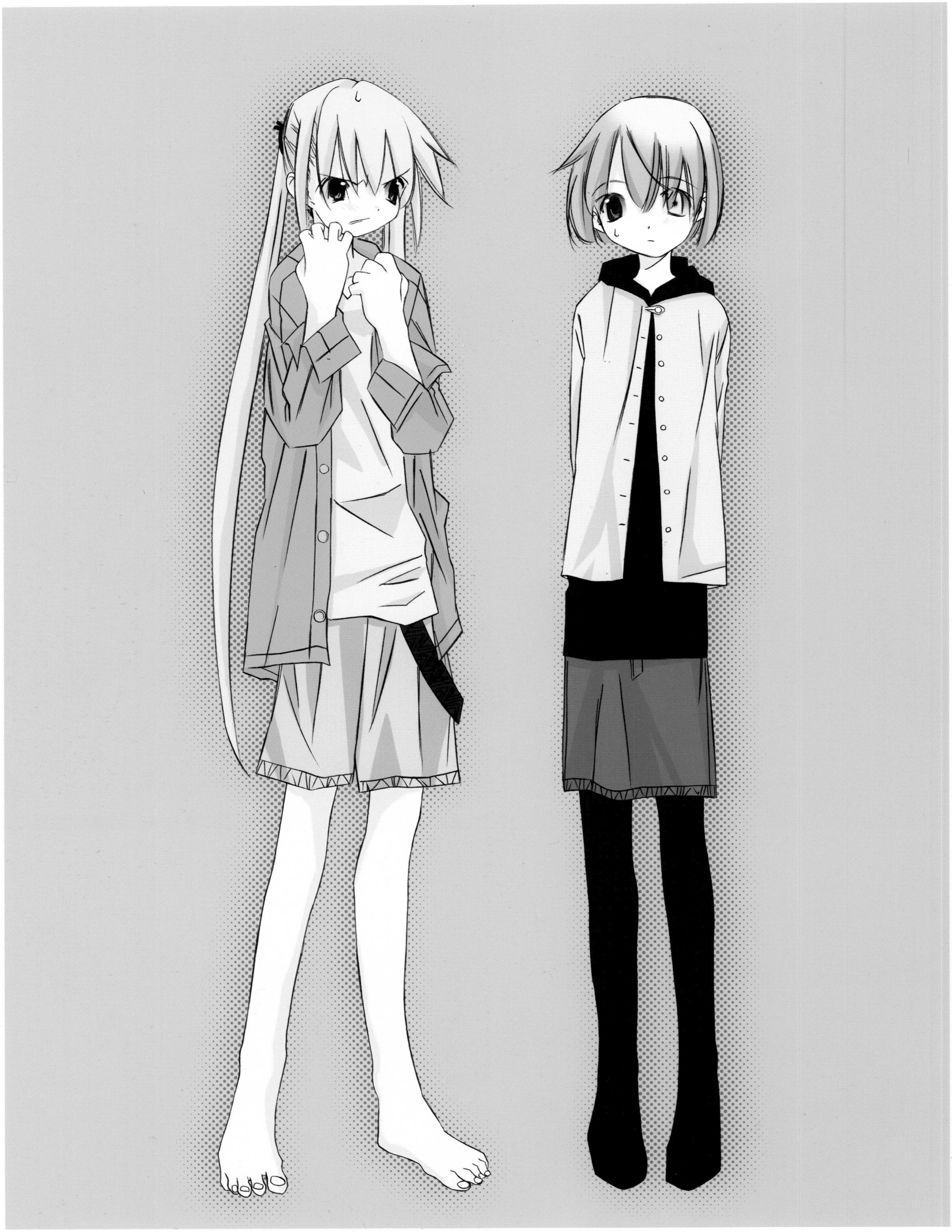

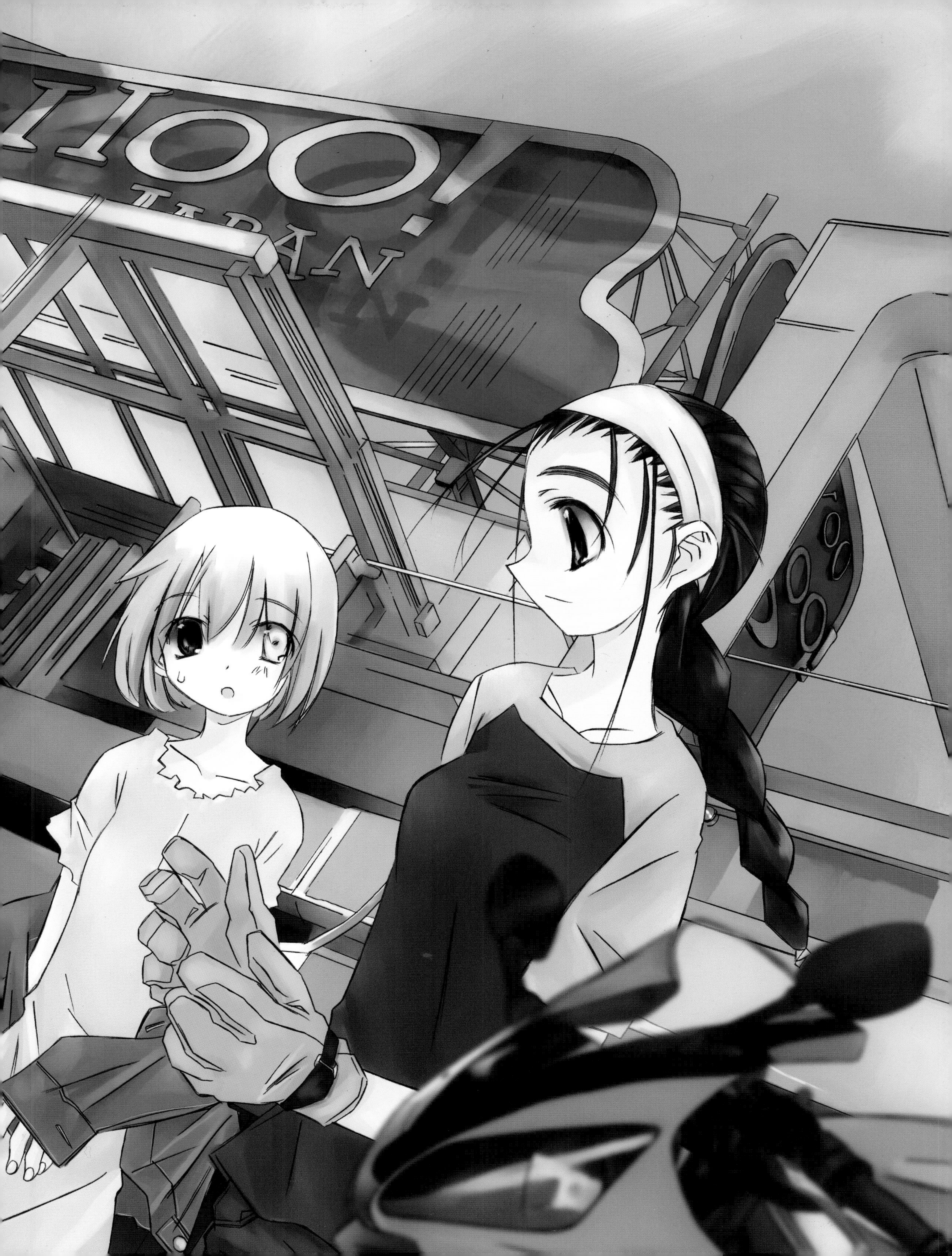
JAPAN

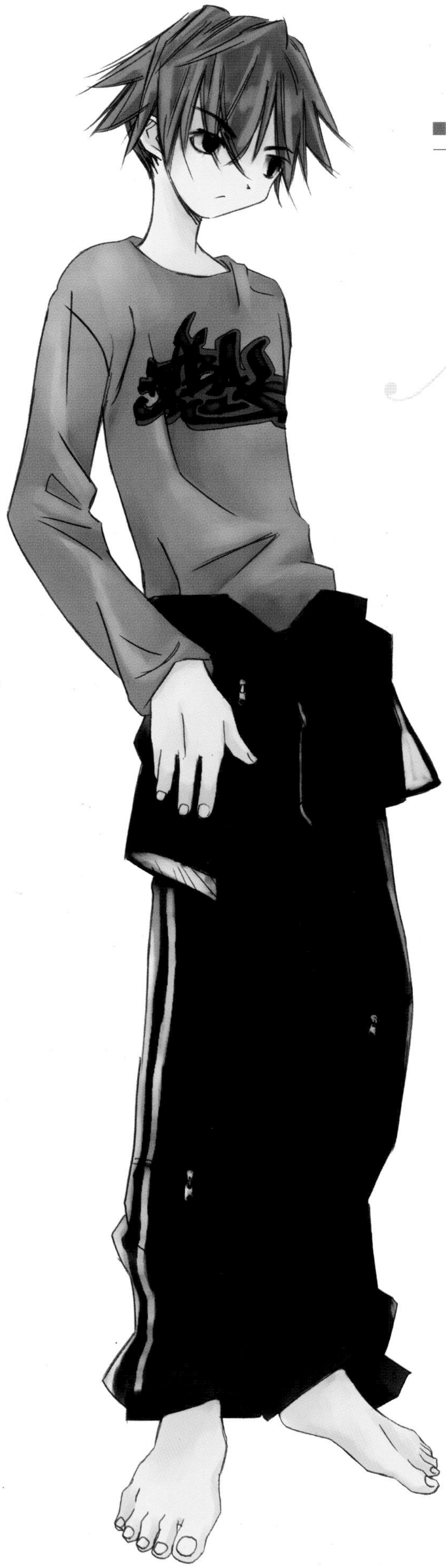

■ Mei Nogisaka

Mei Nogisaka

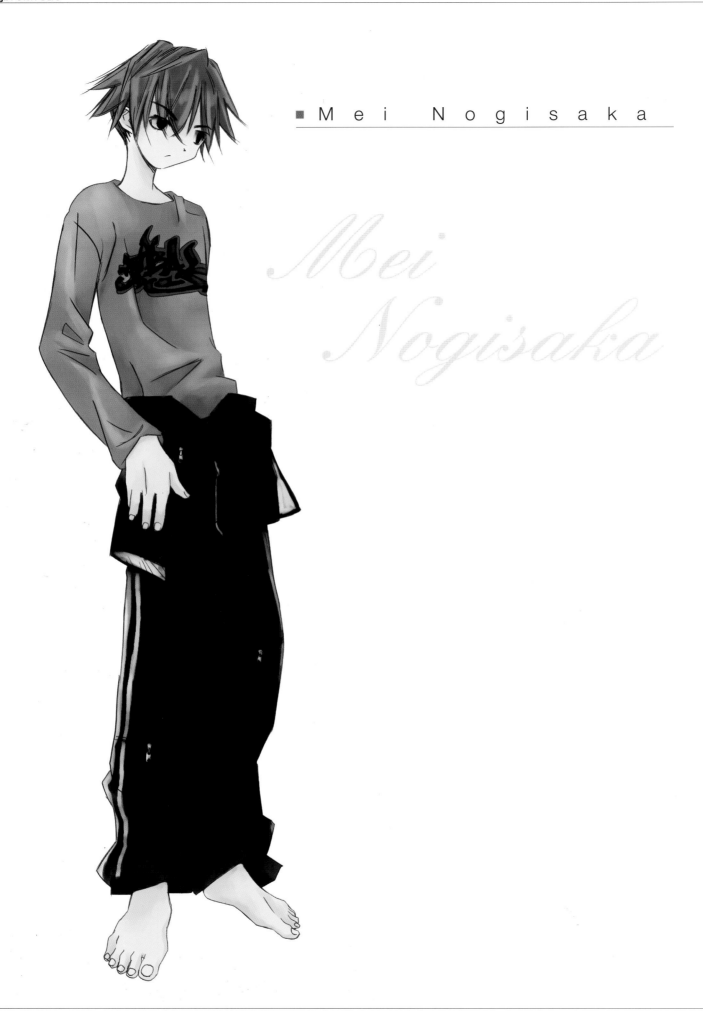

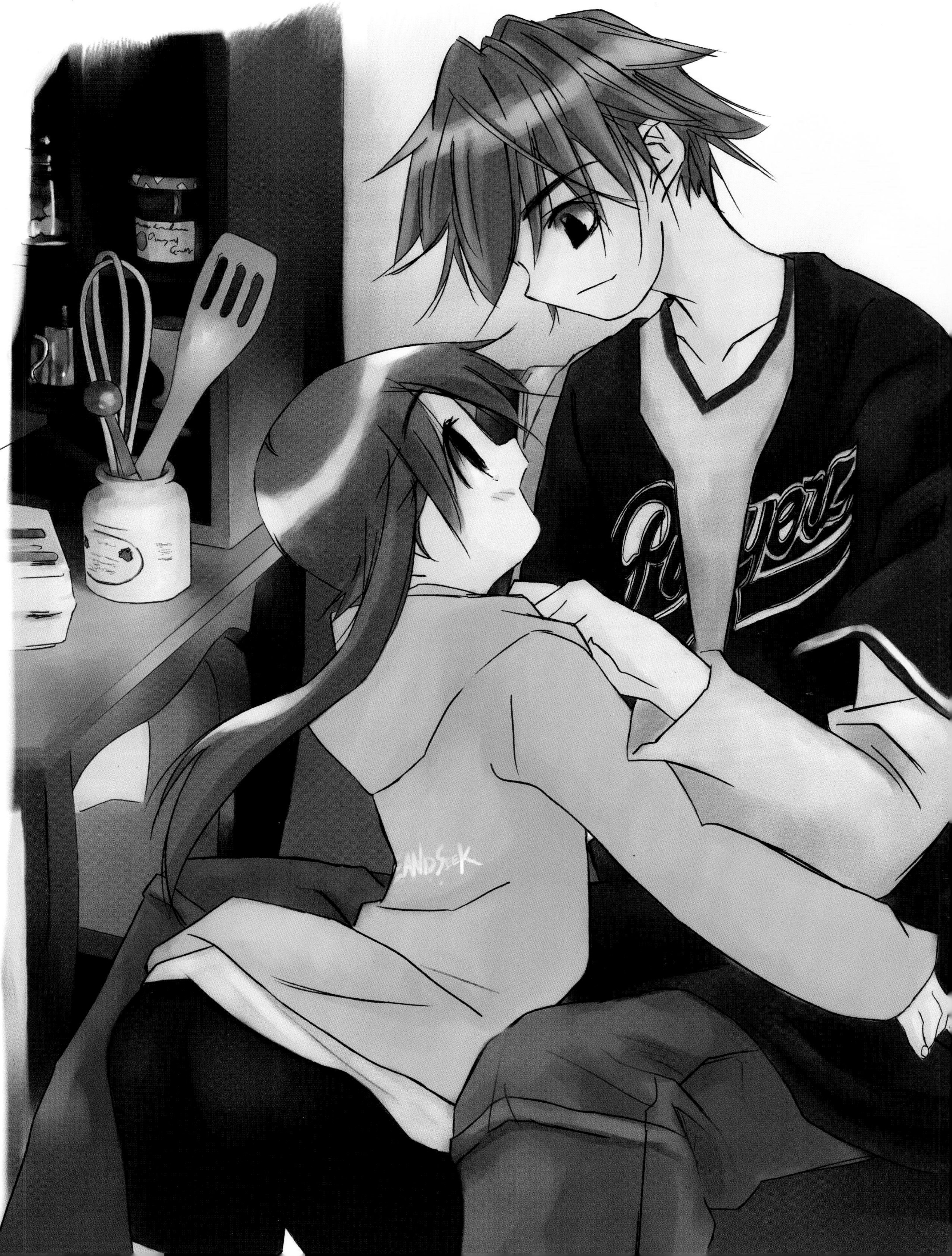

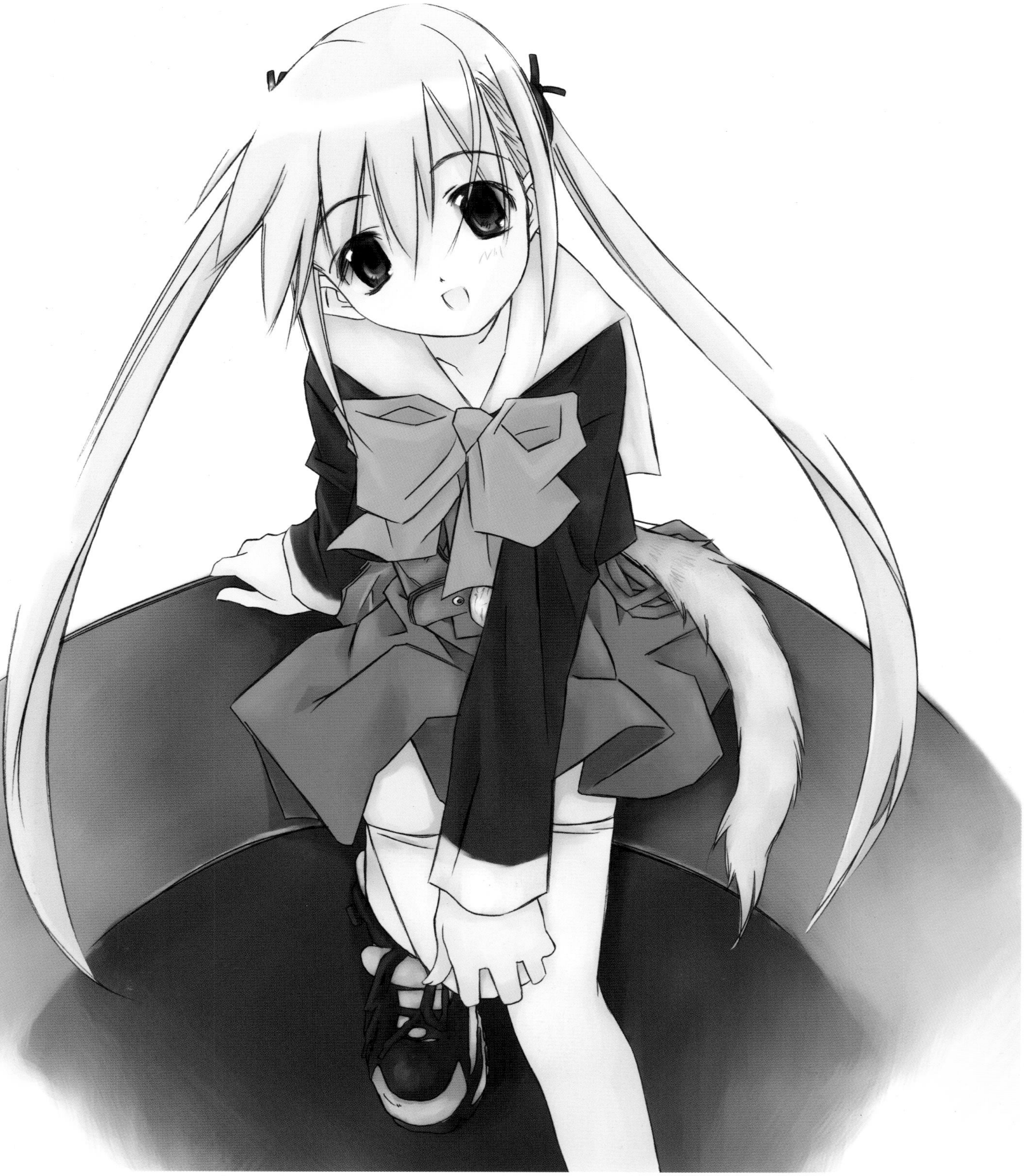

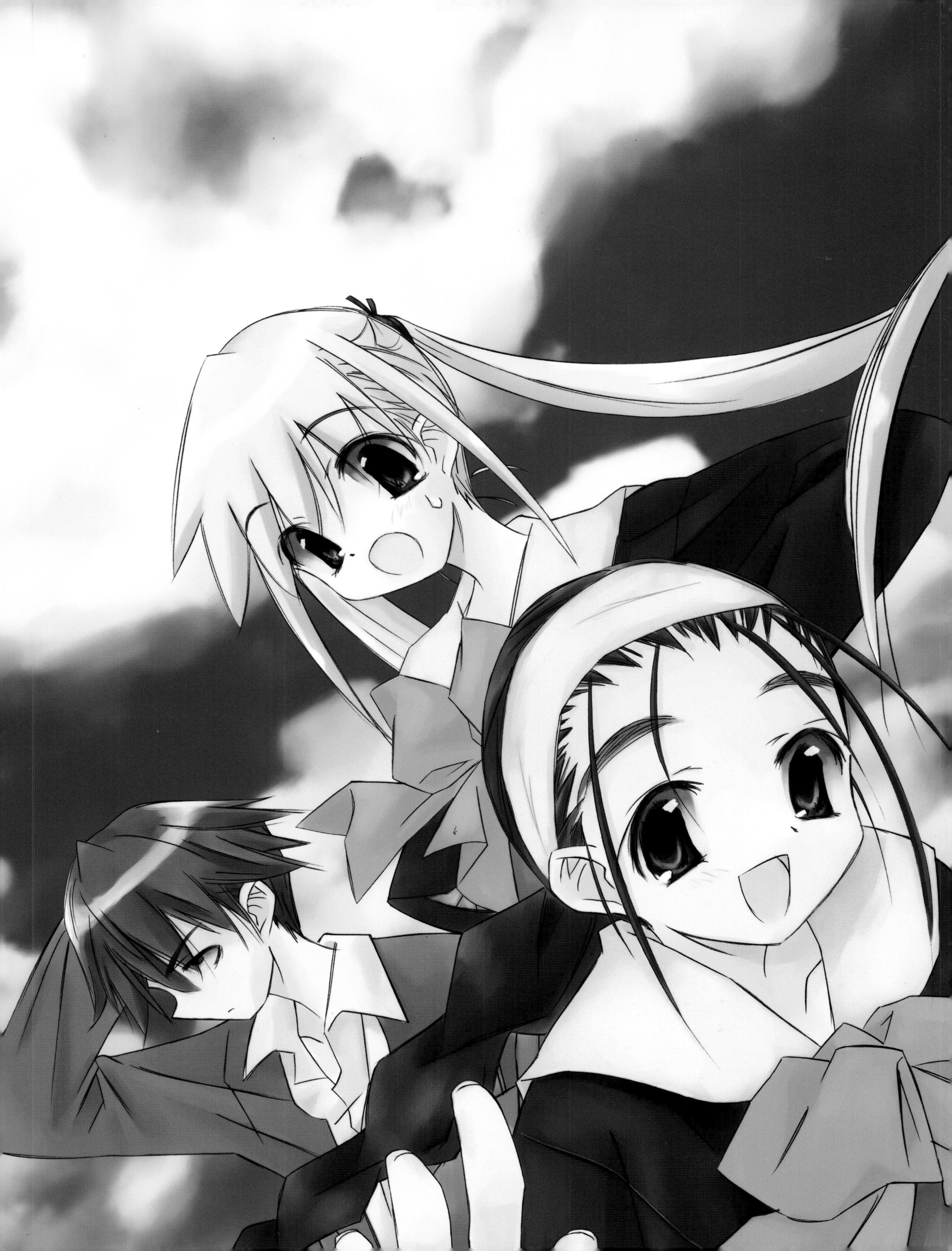

Sakiko Fujima

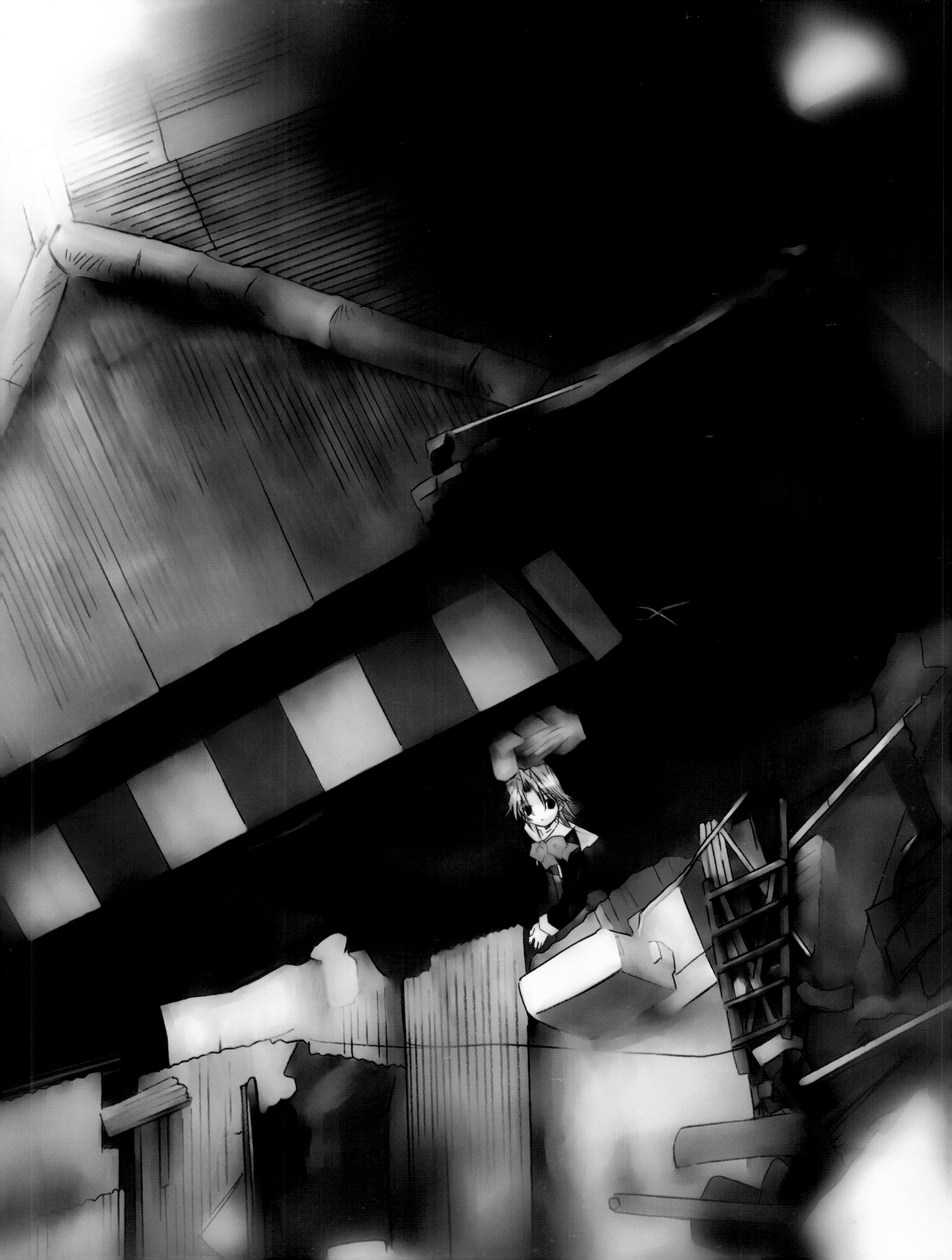

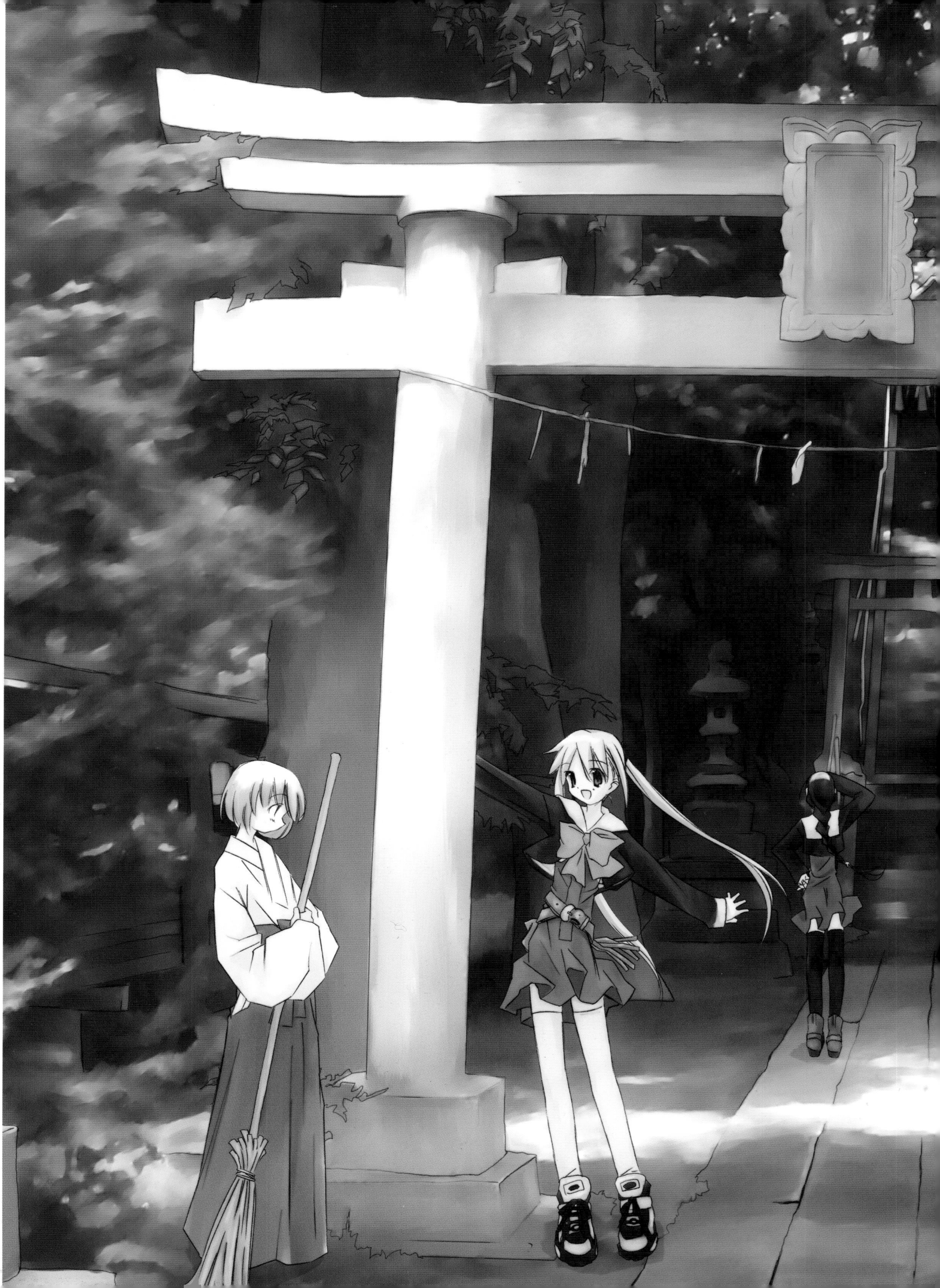

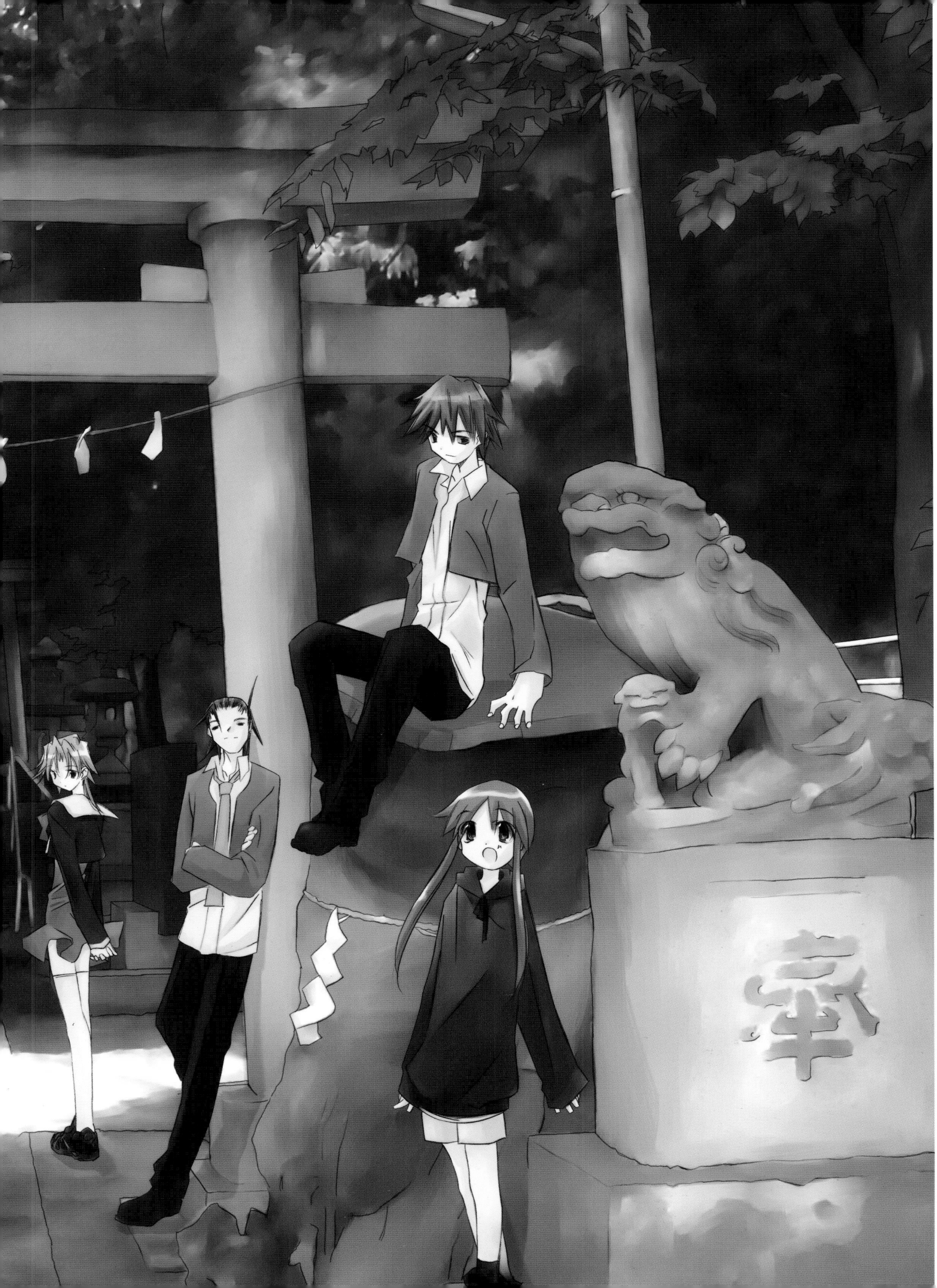

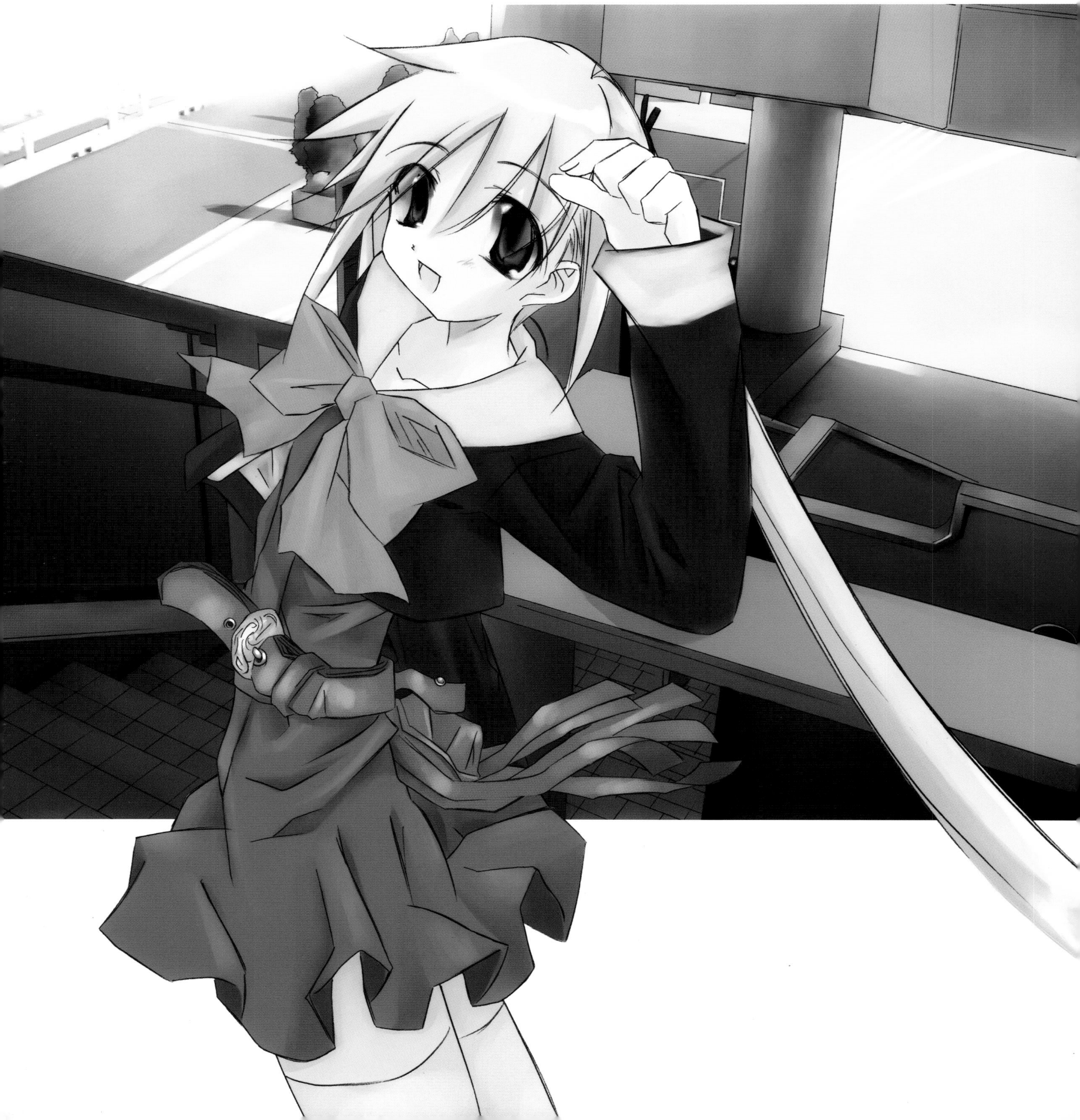

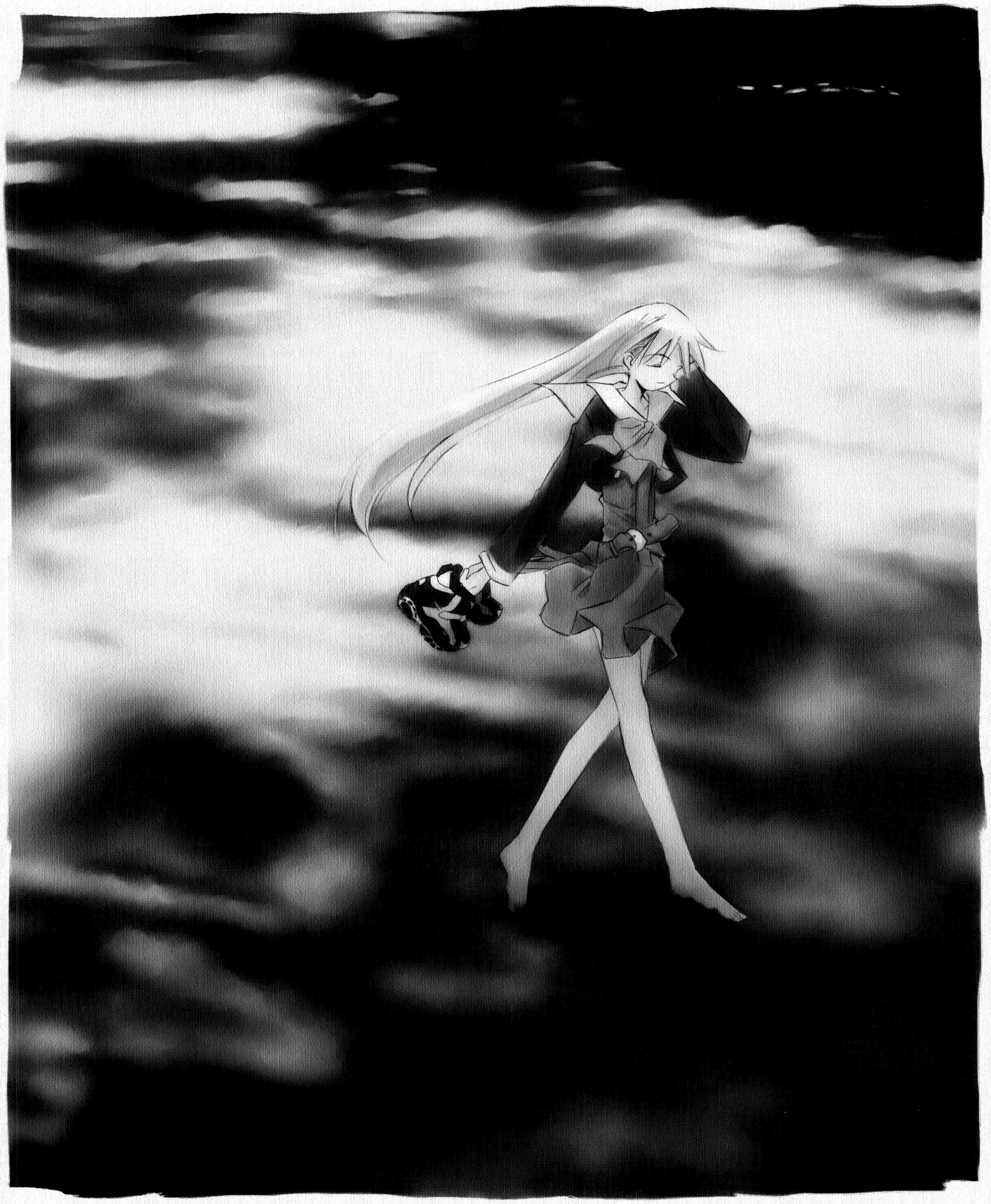

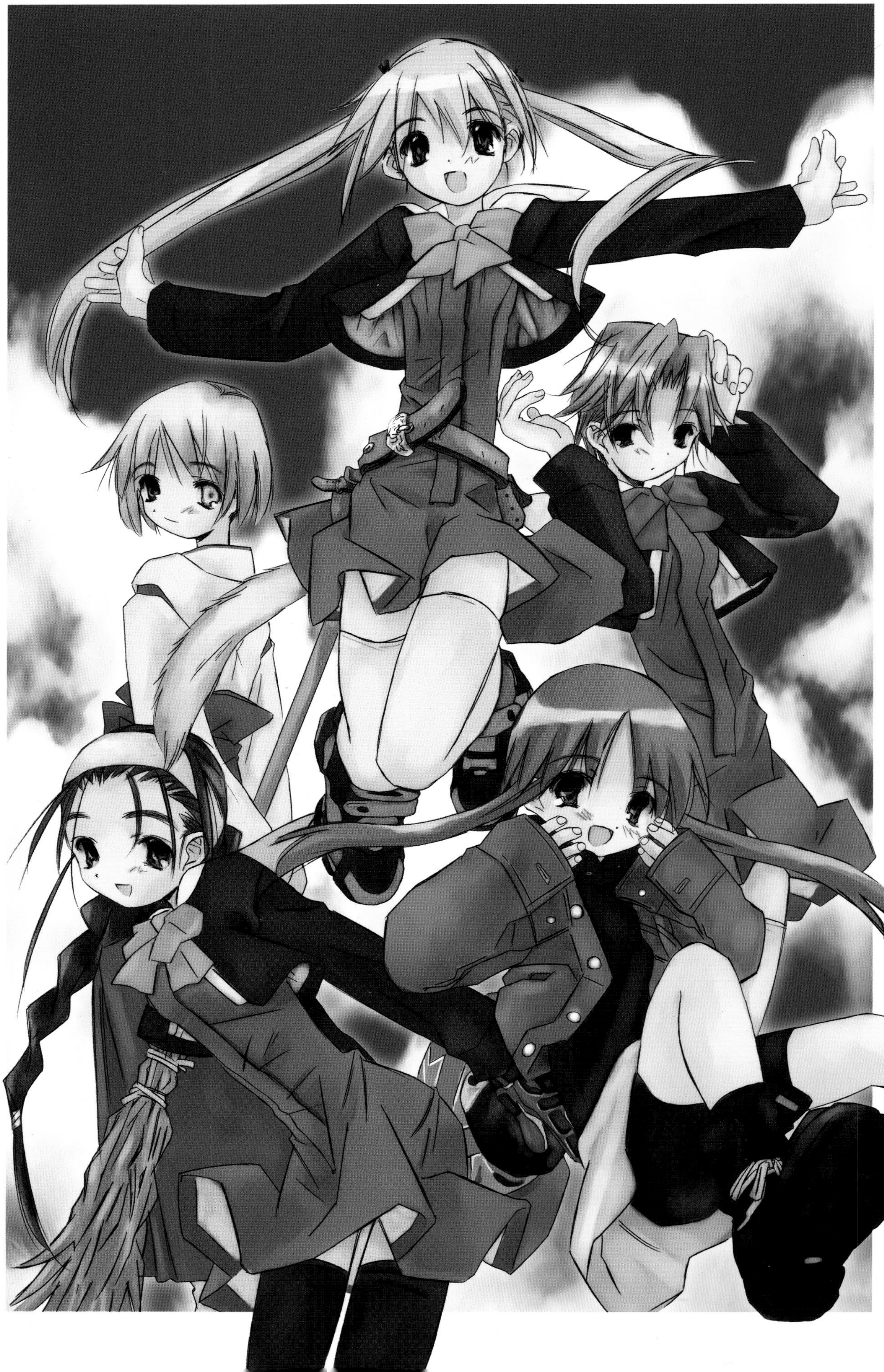

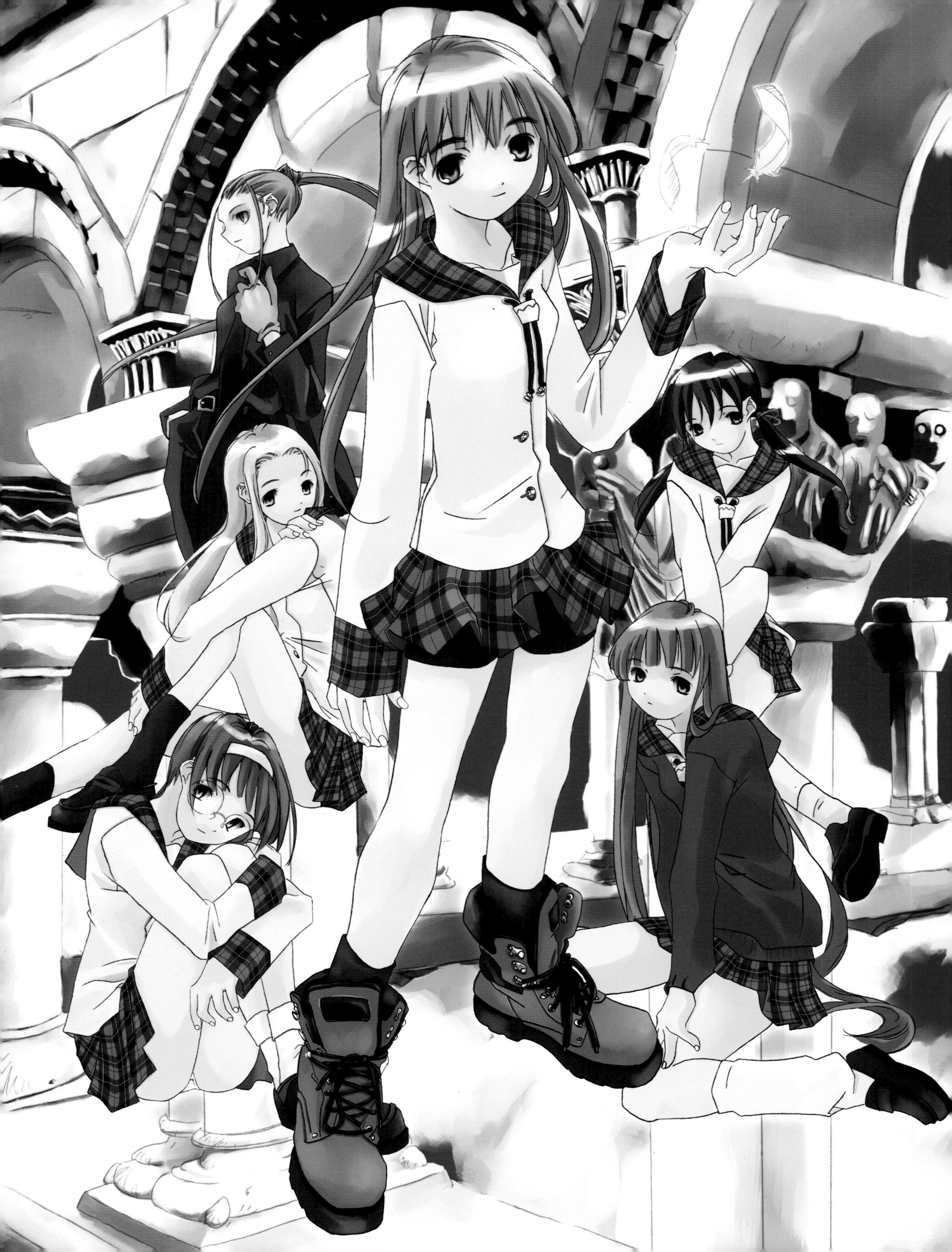

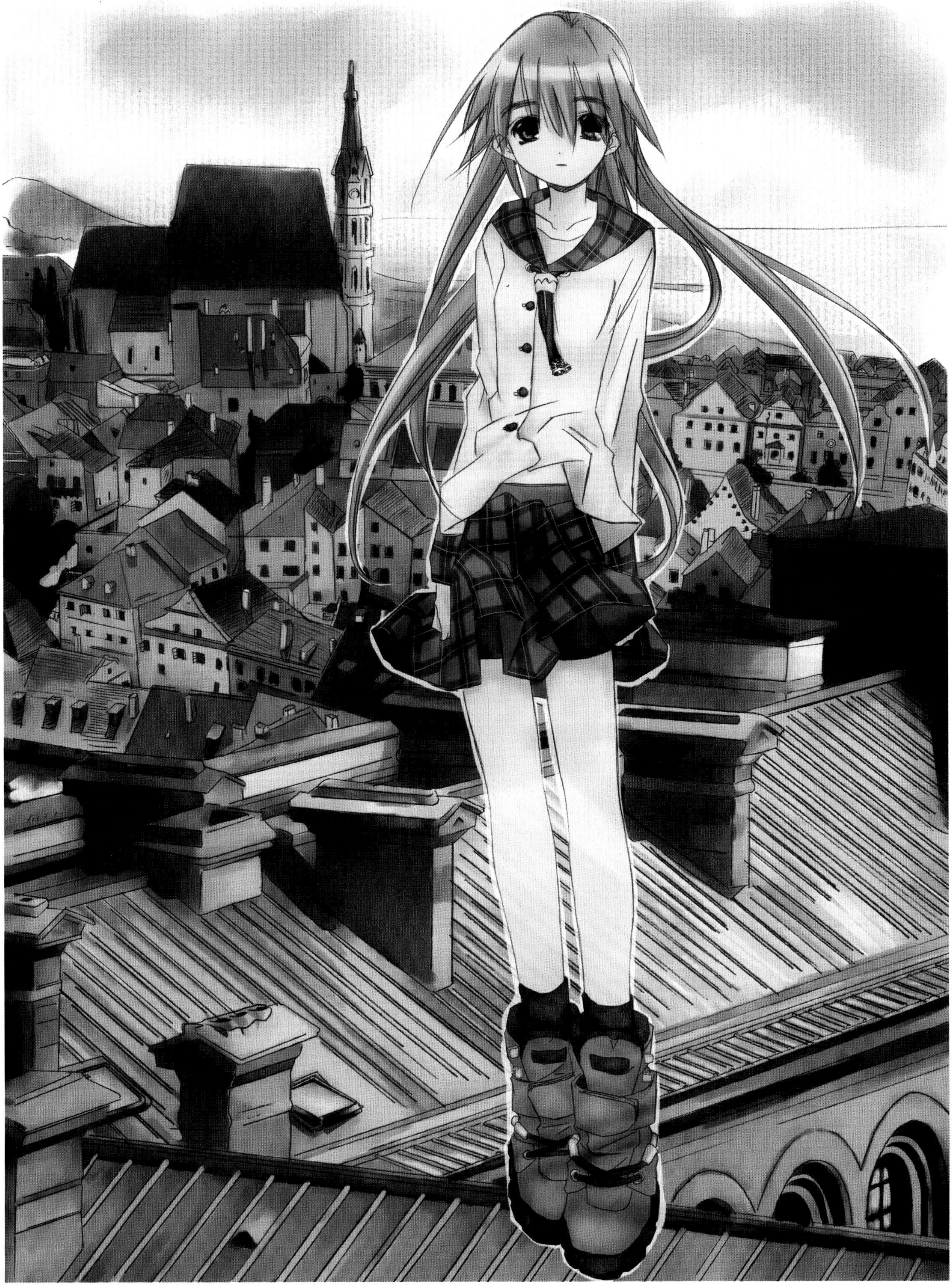

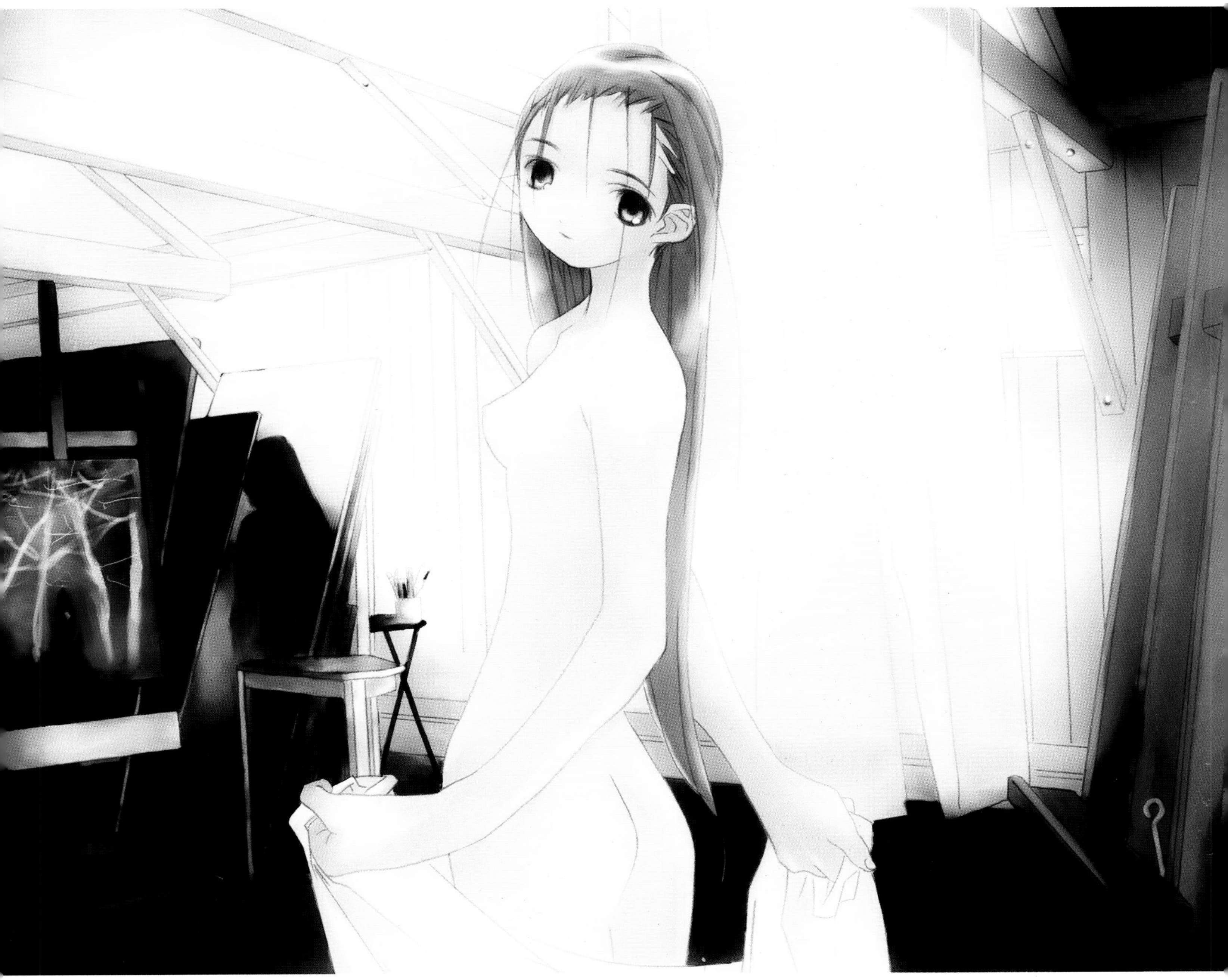

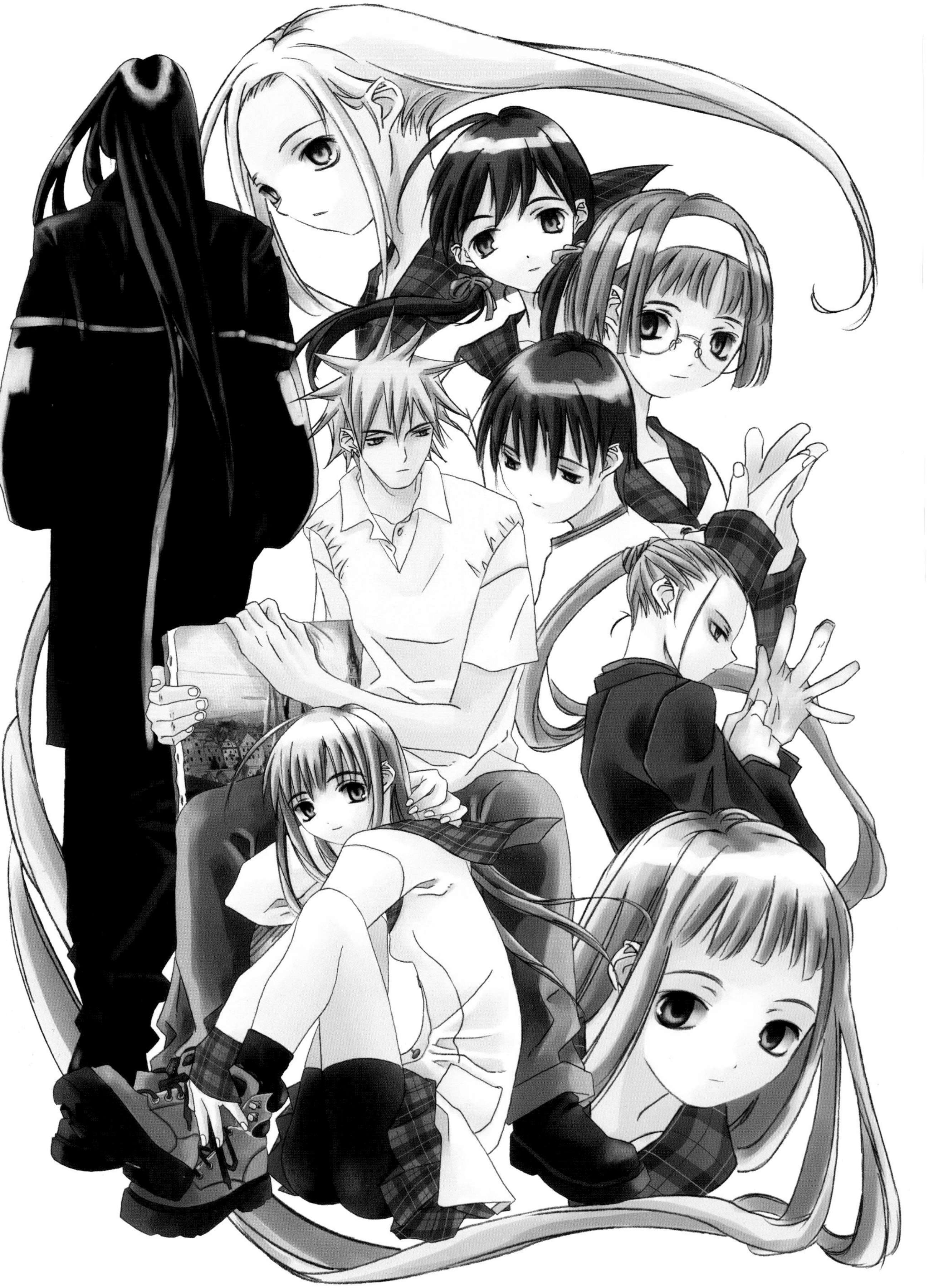

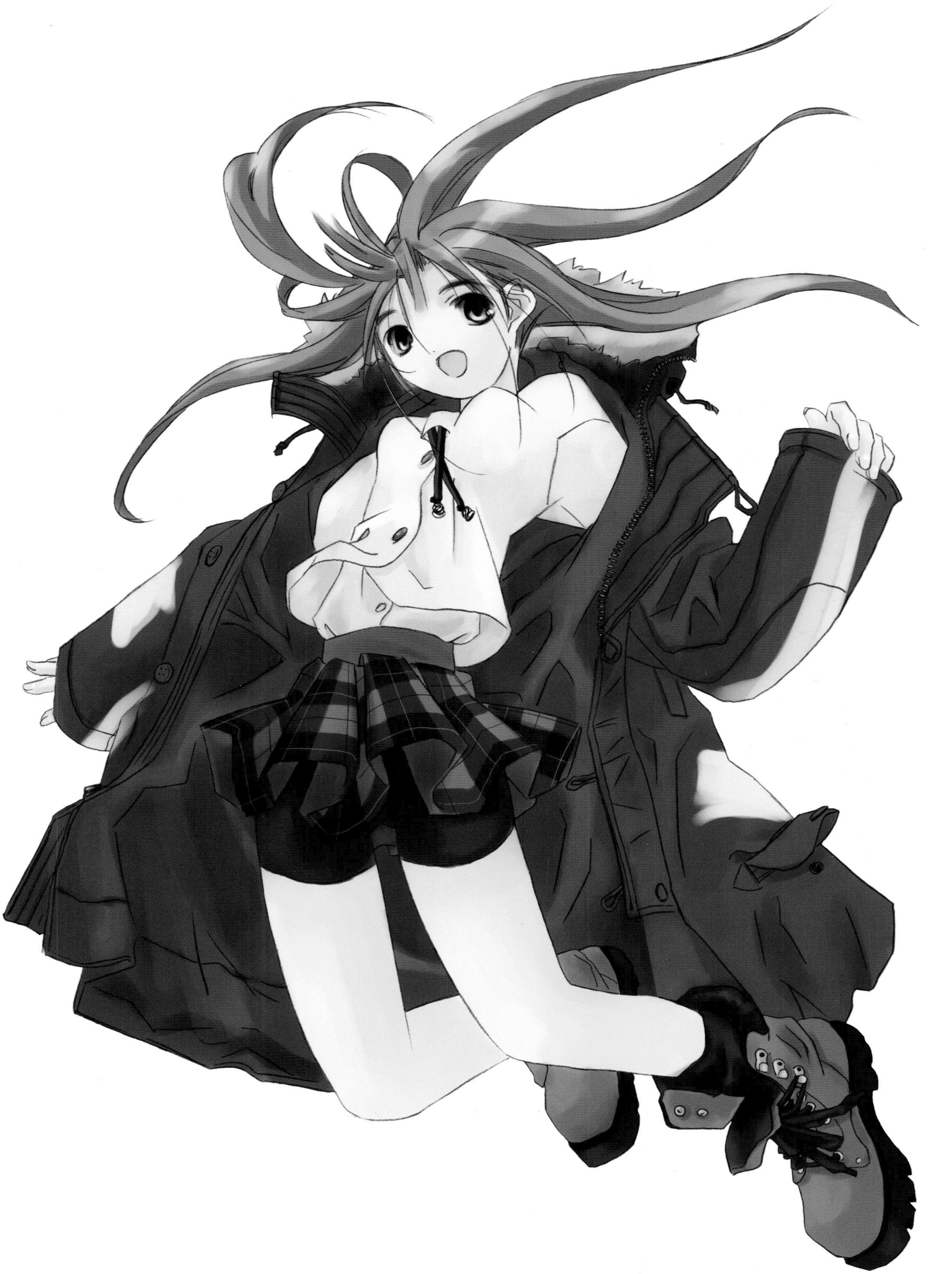

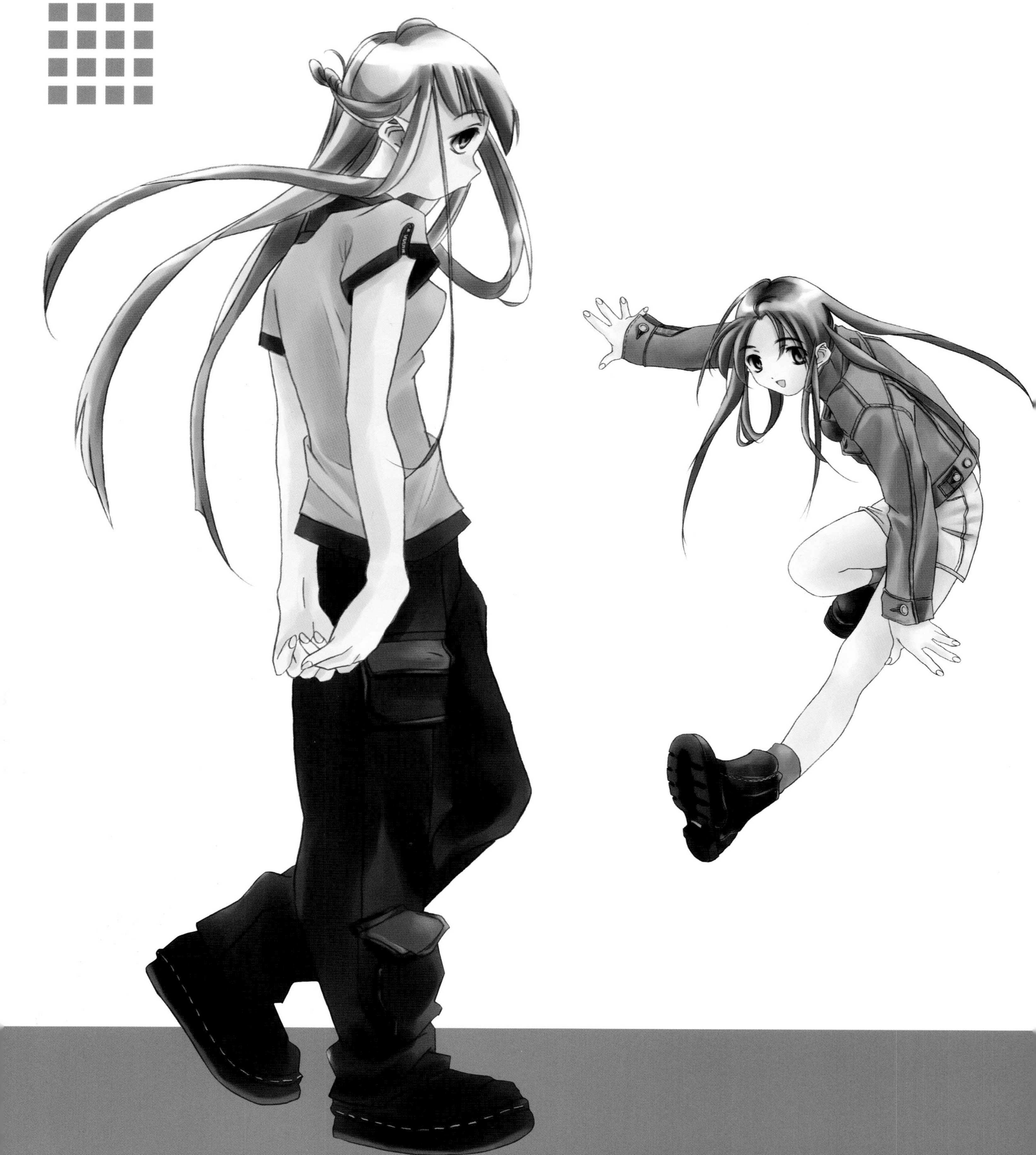

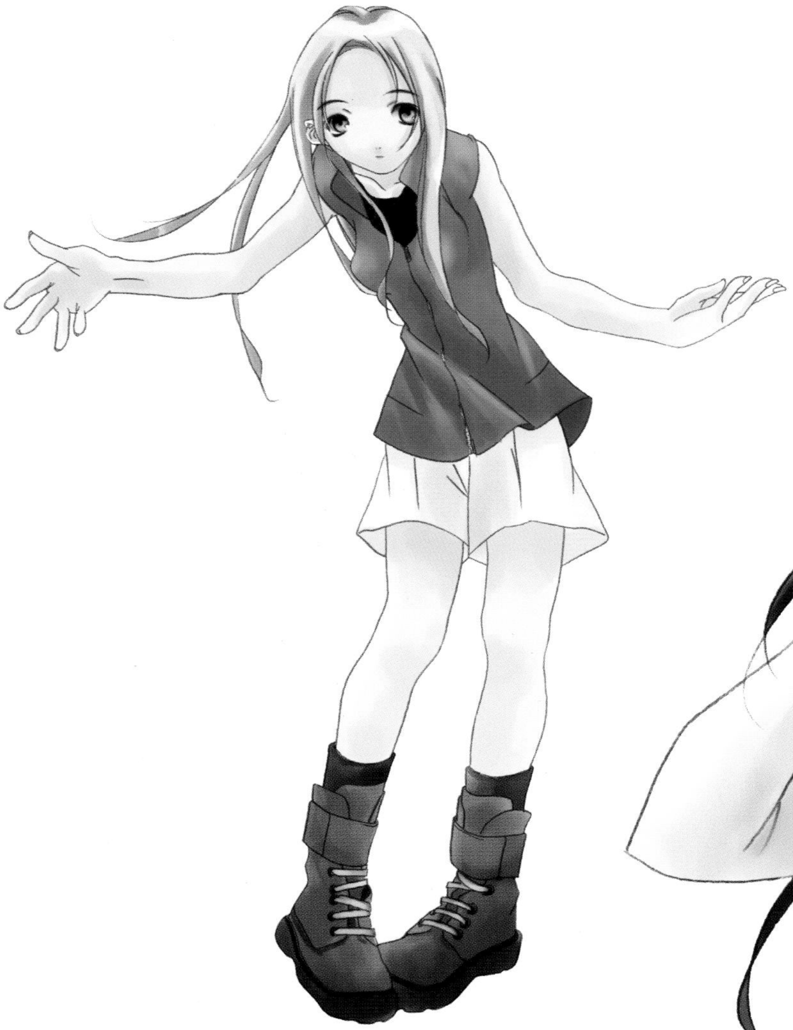

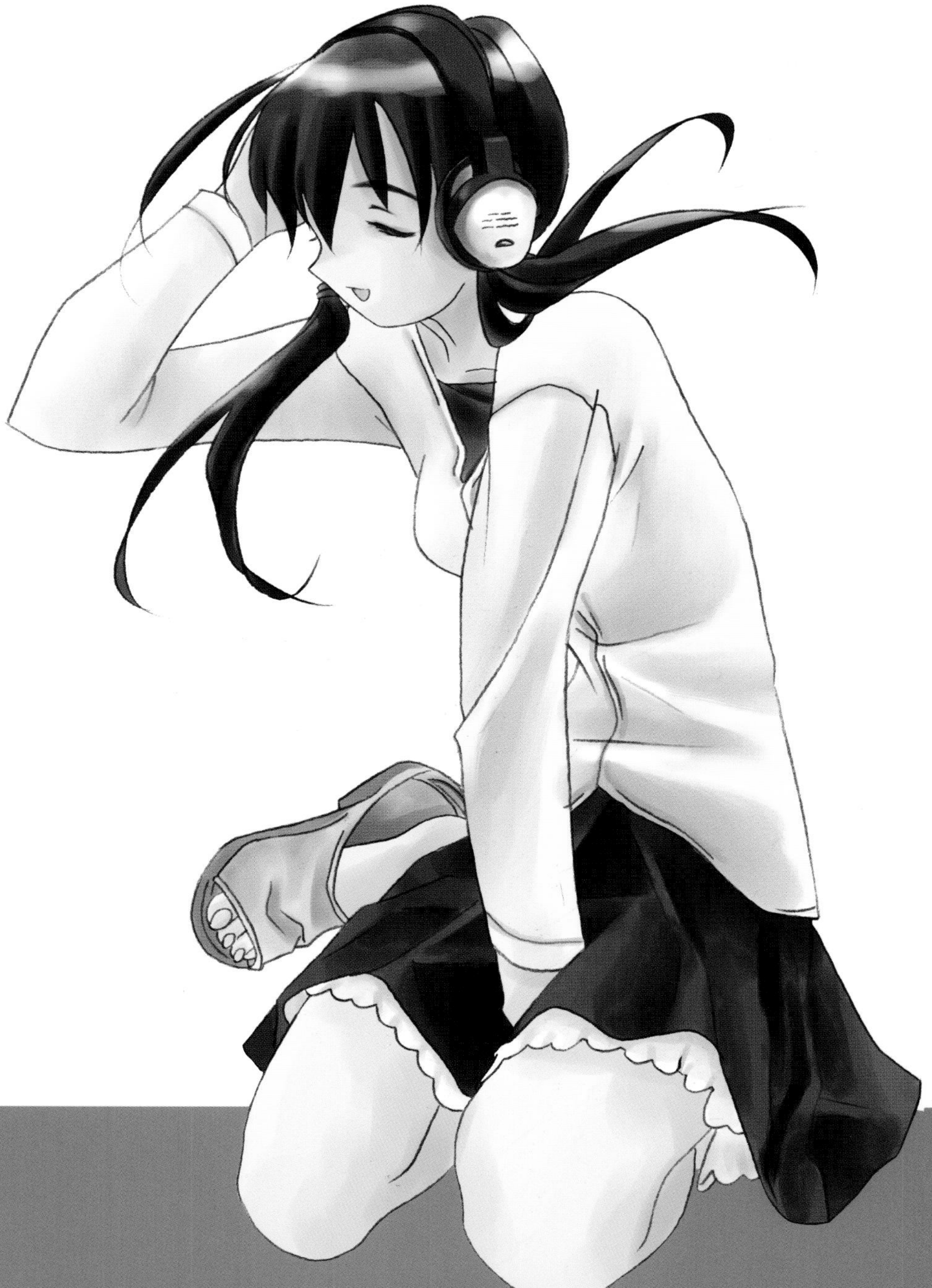

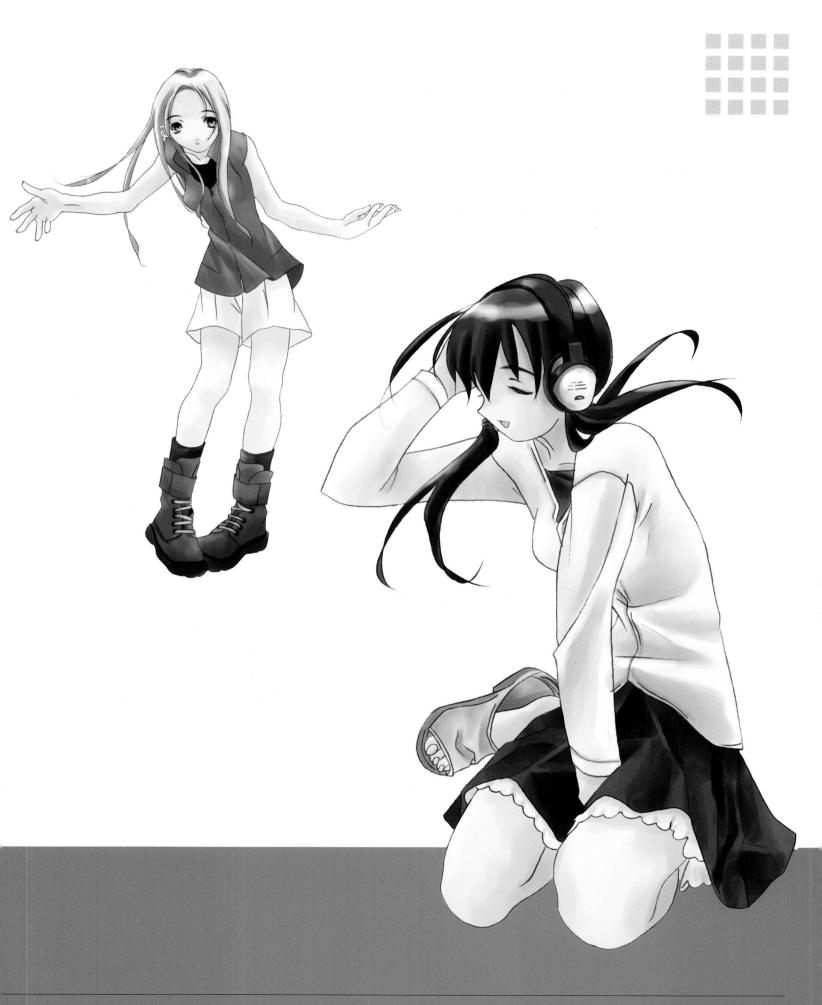

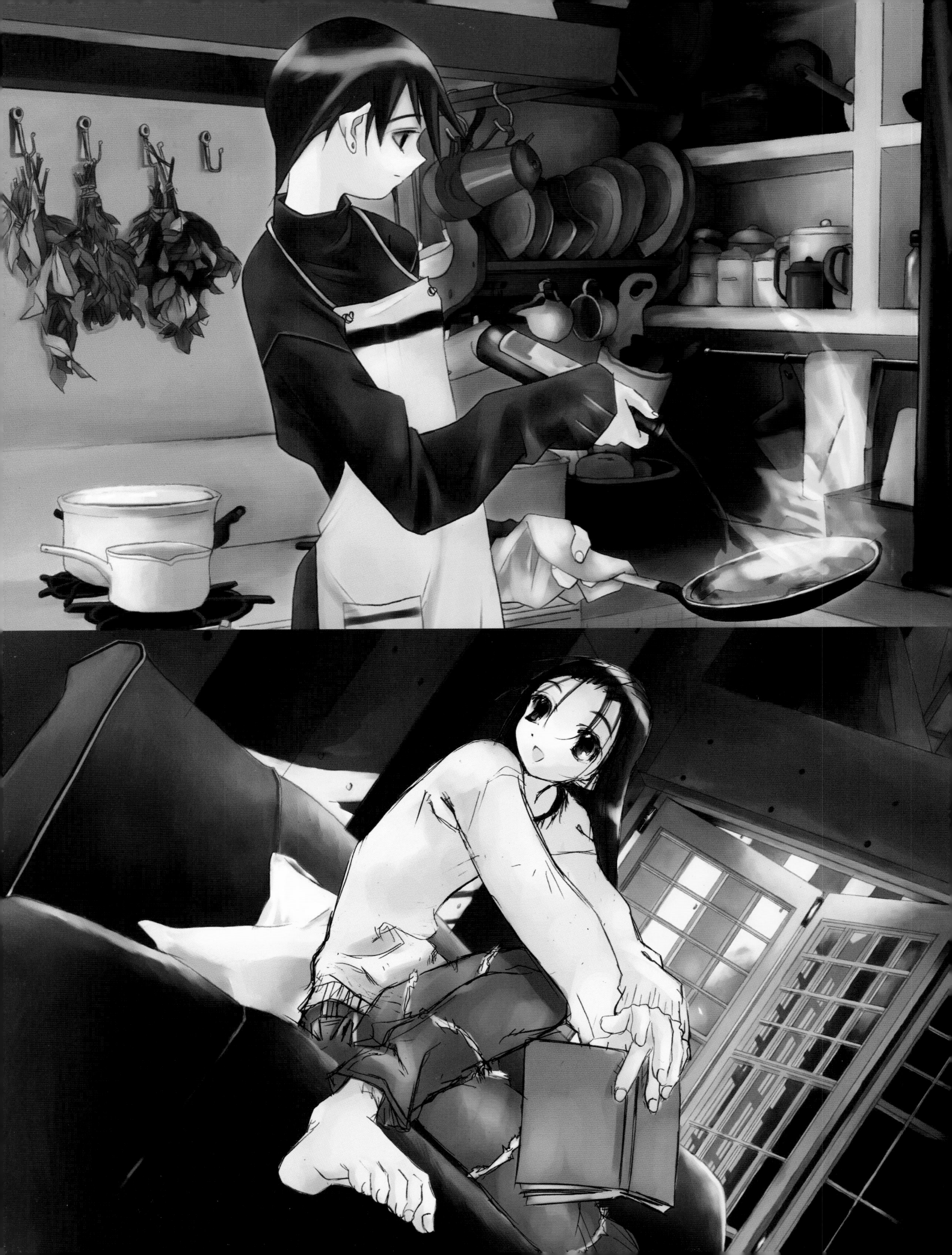

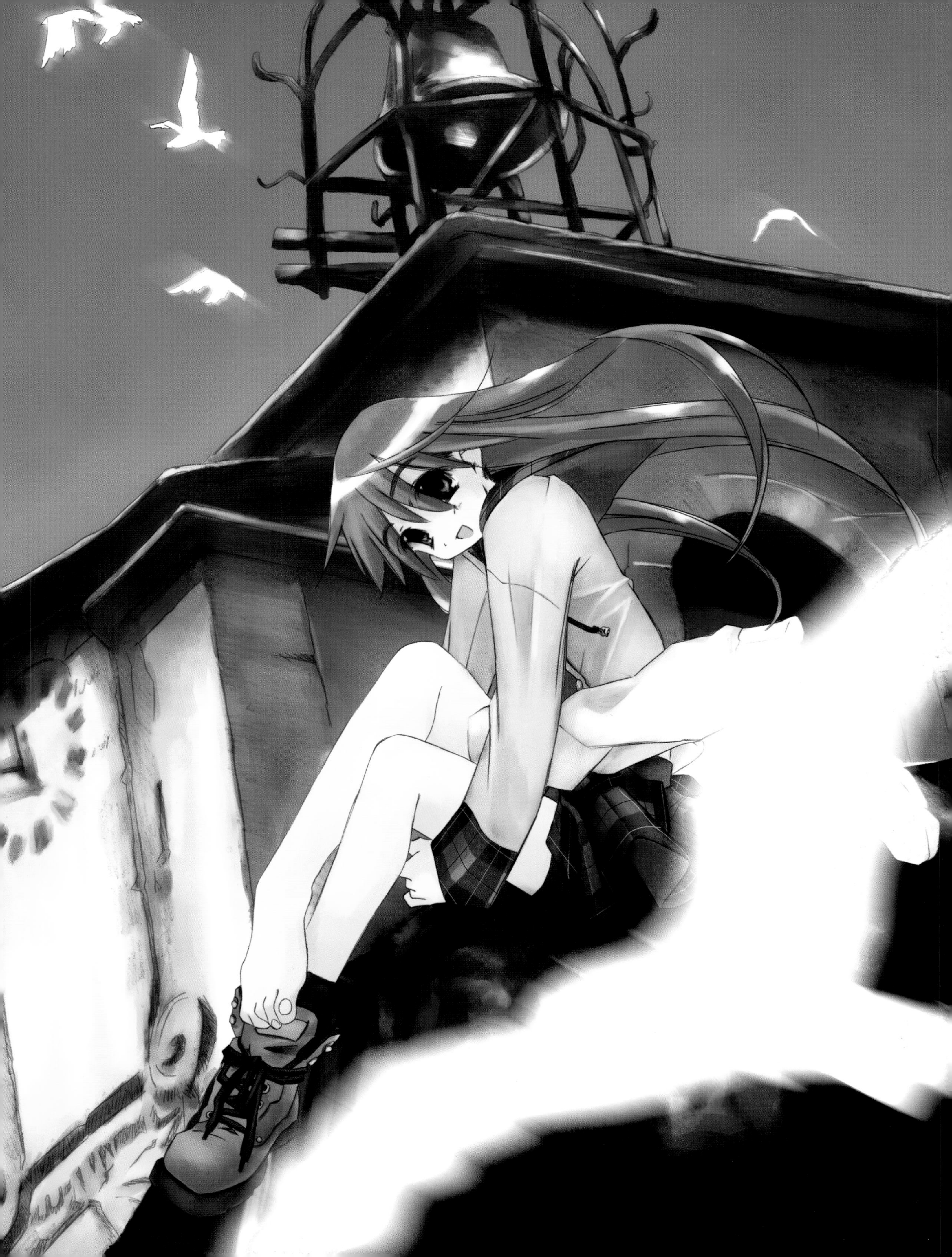

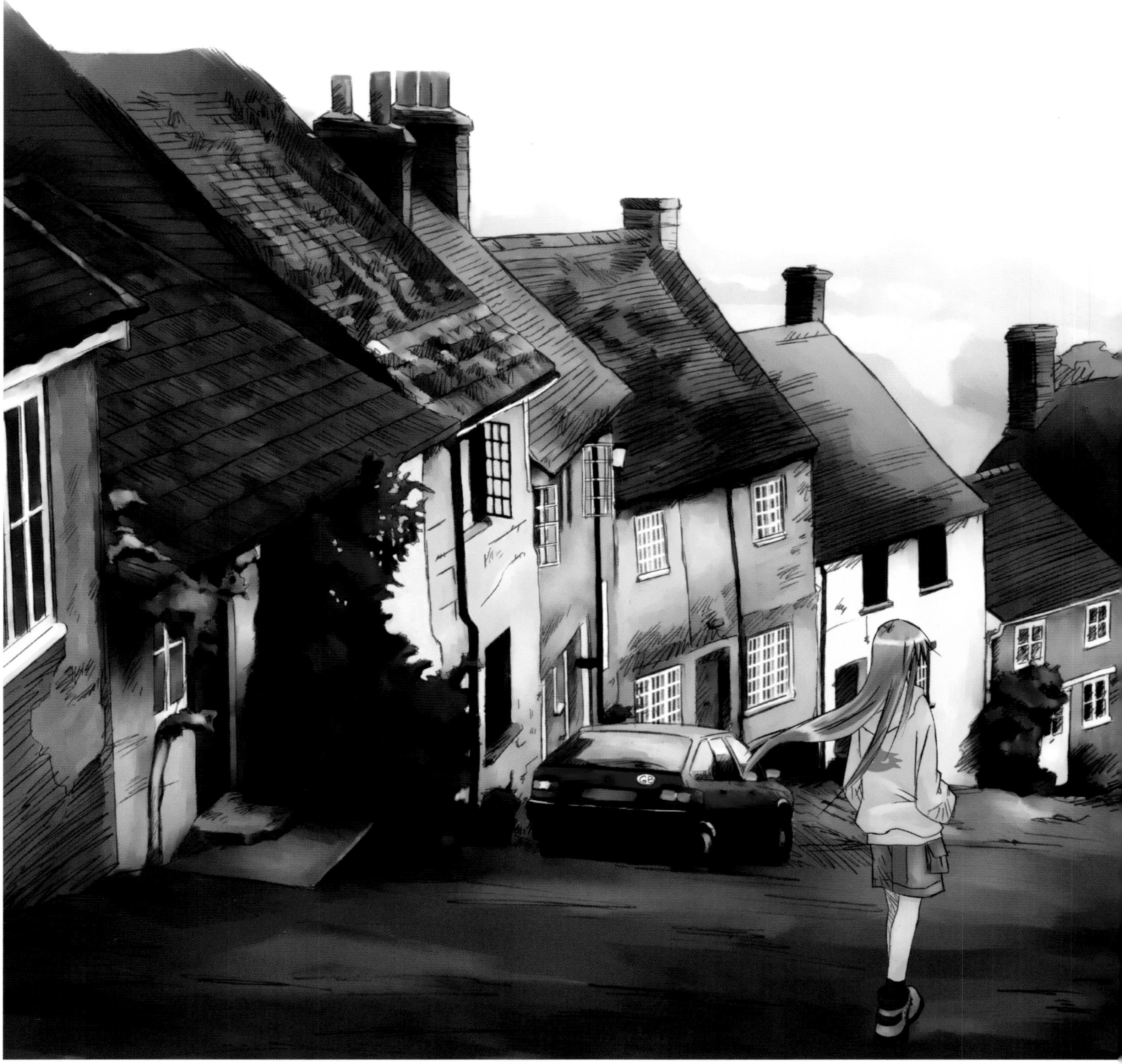

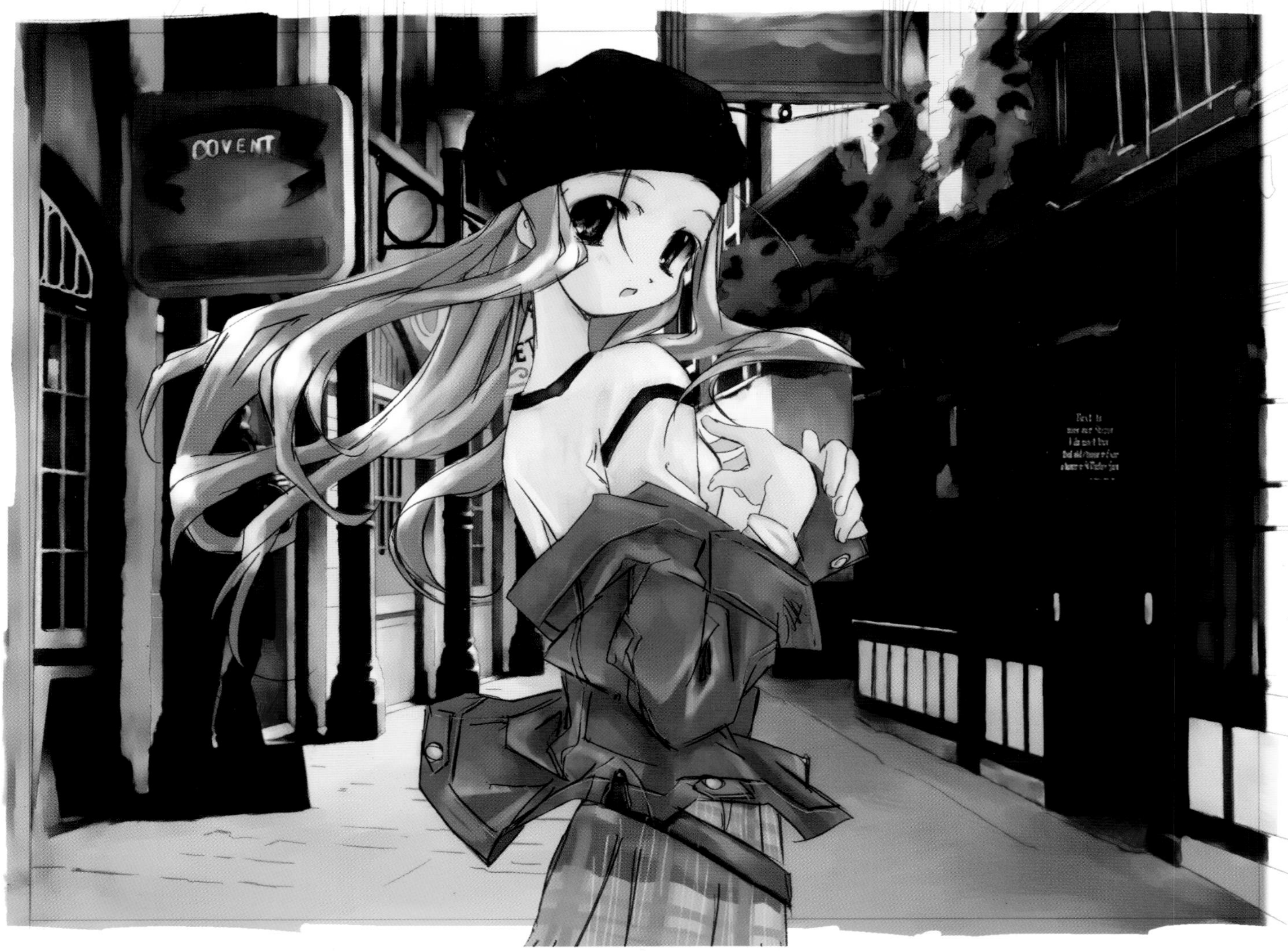
COVENT

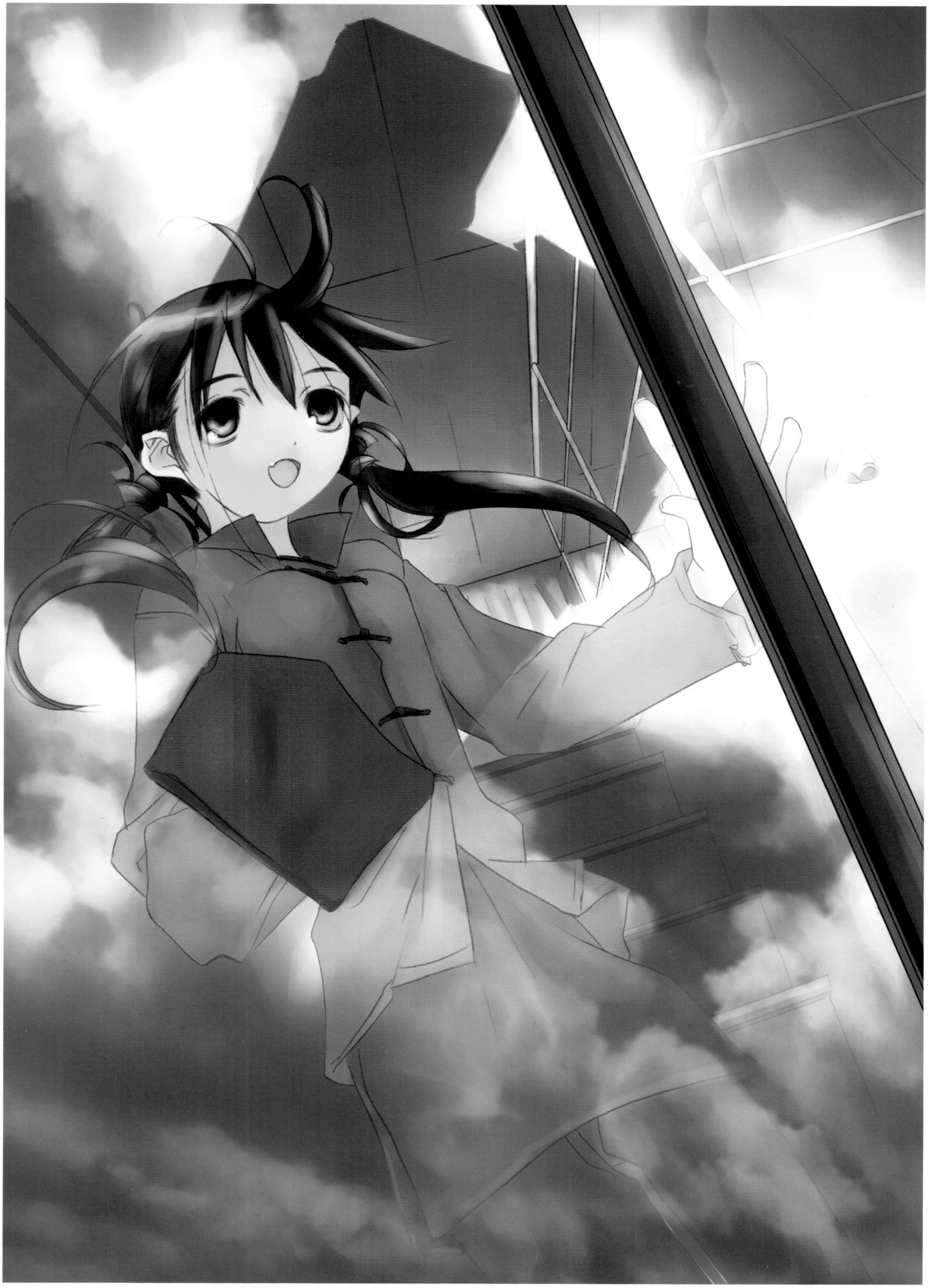

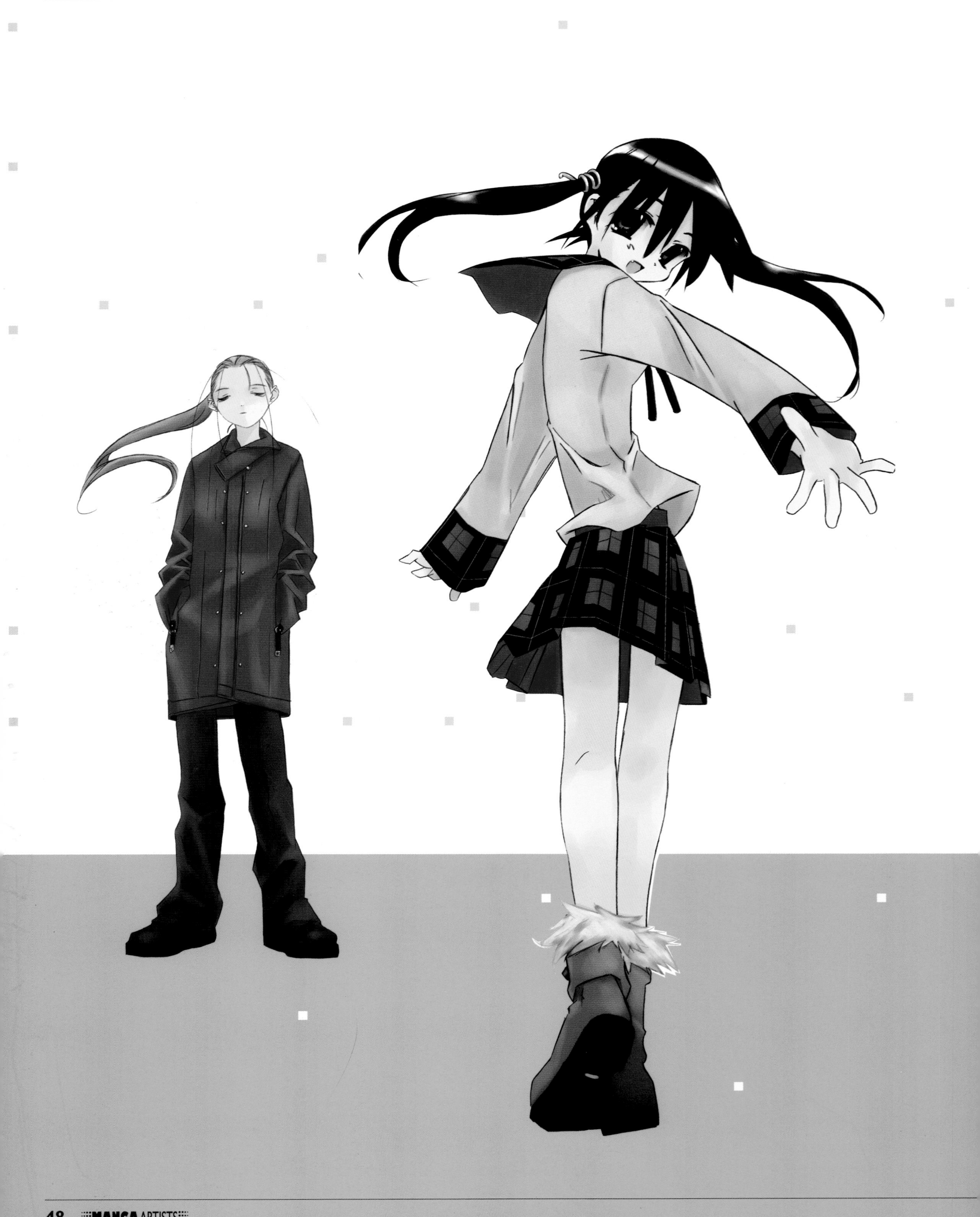

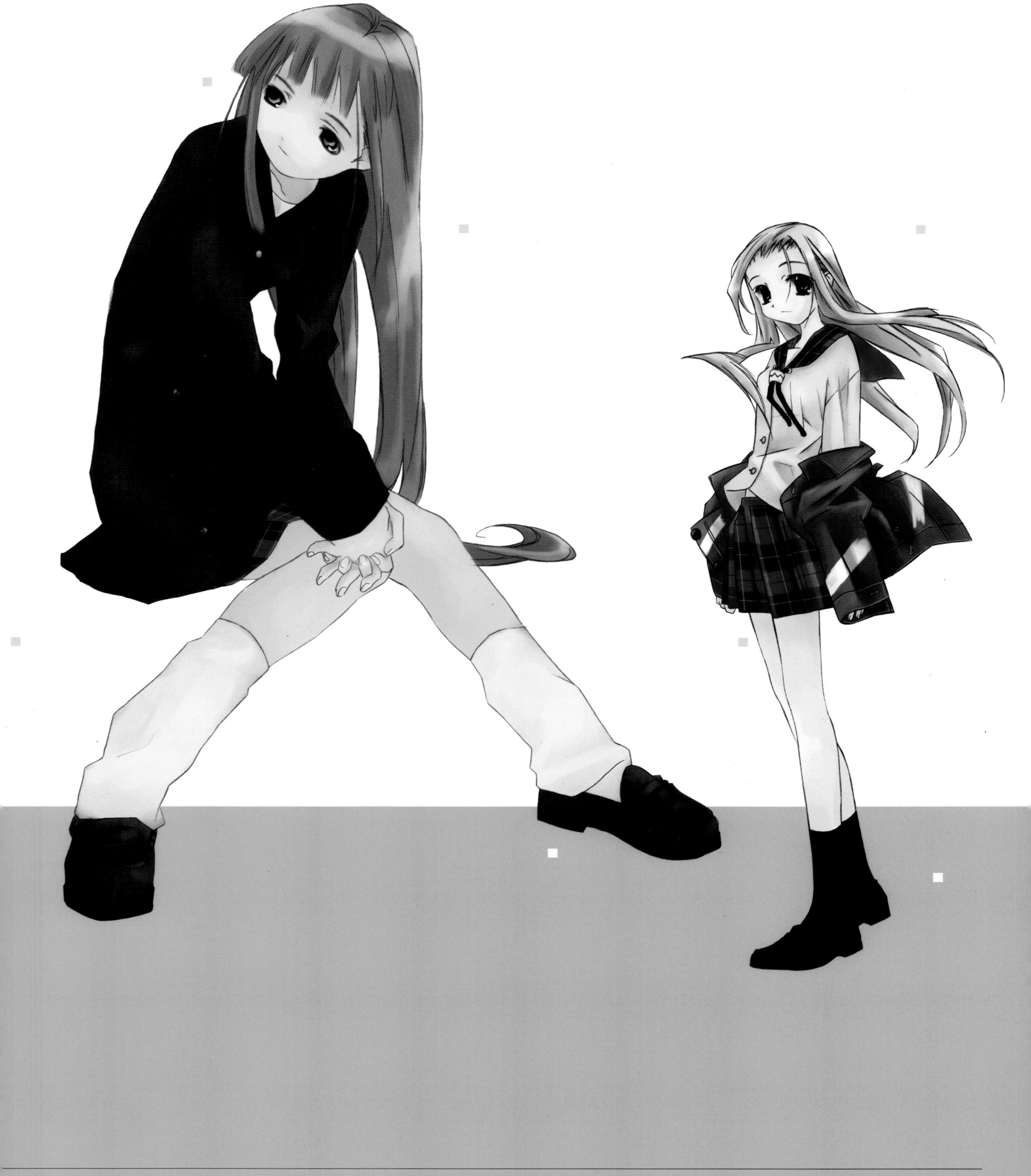

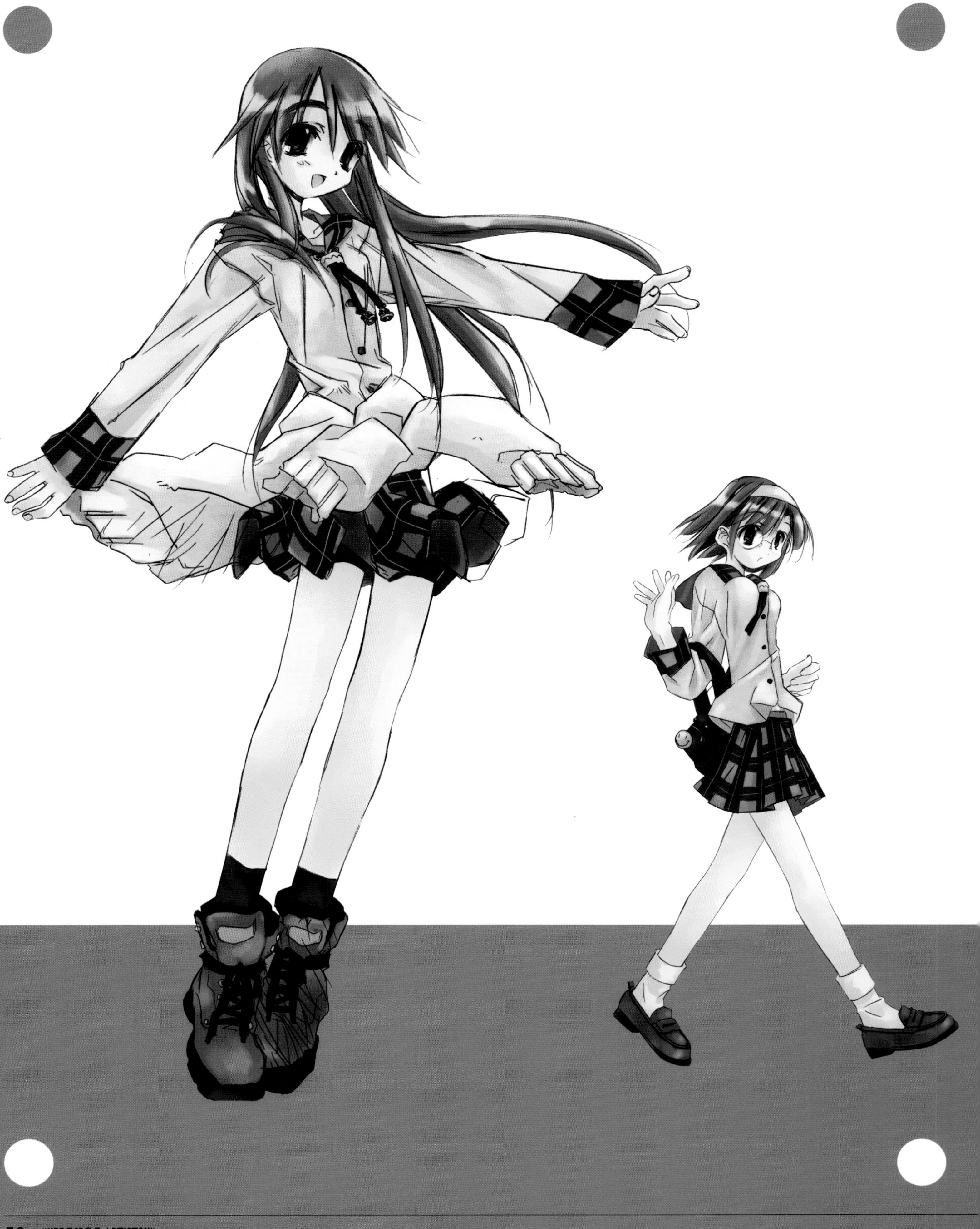

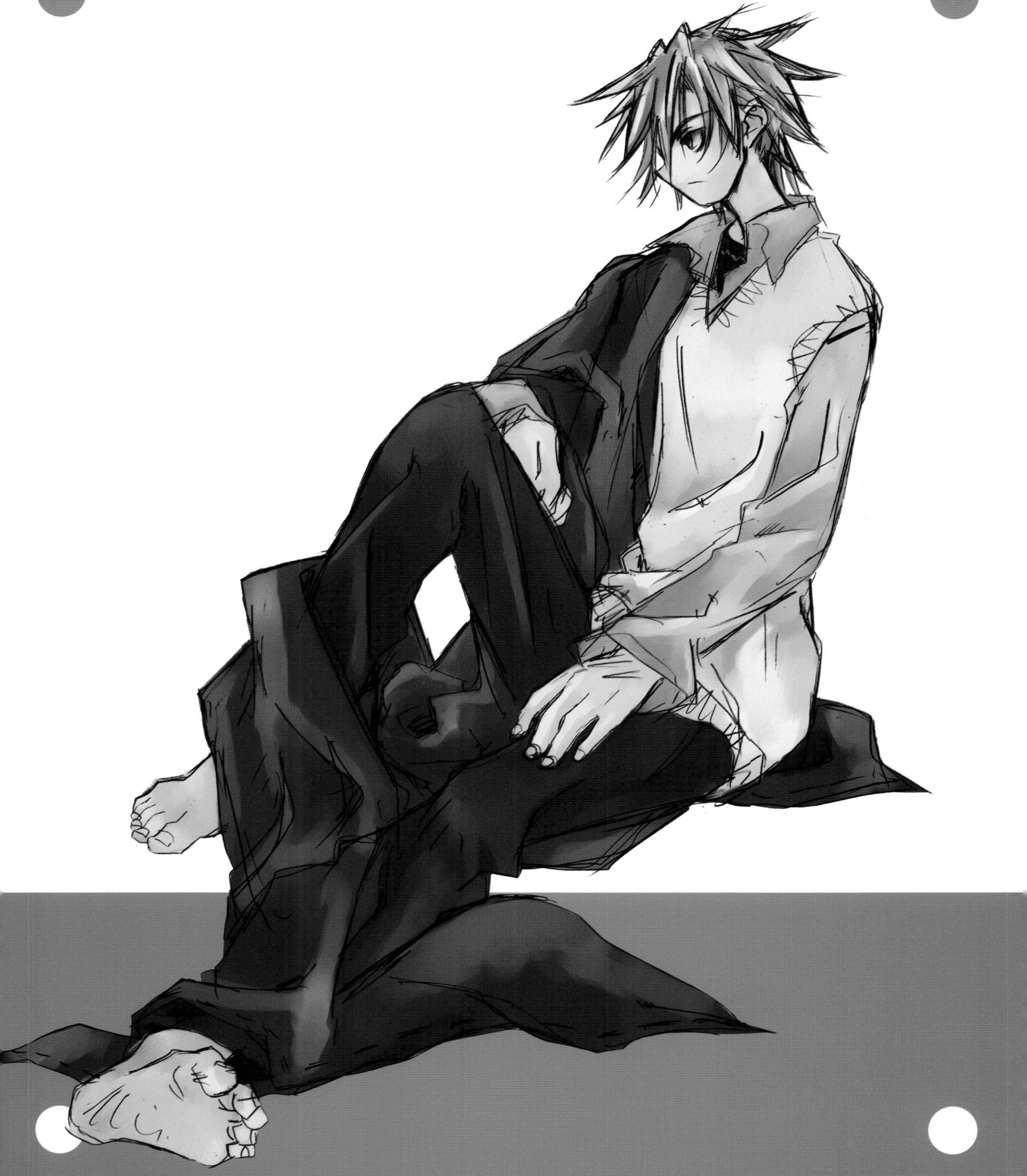

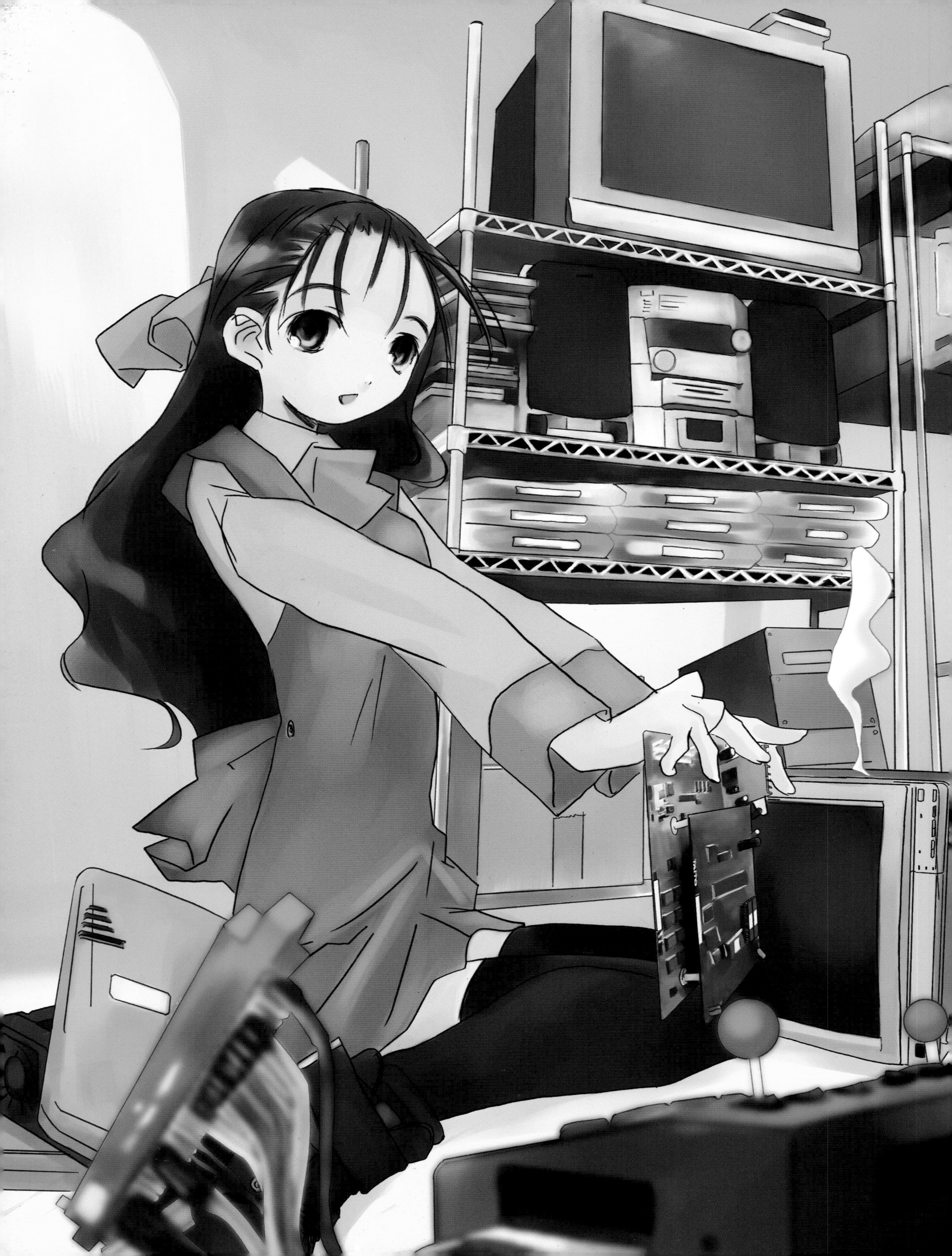

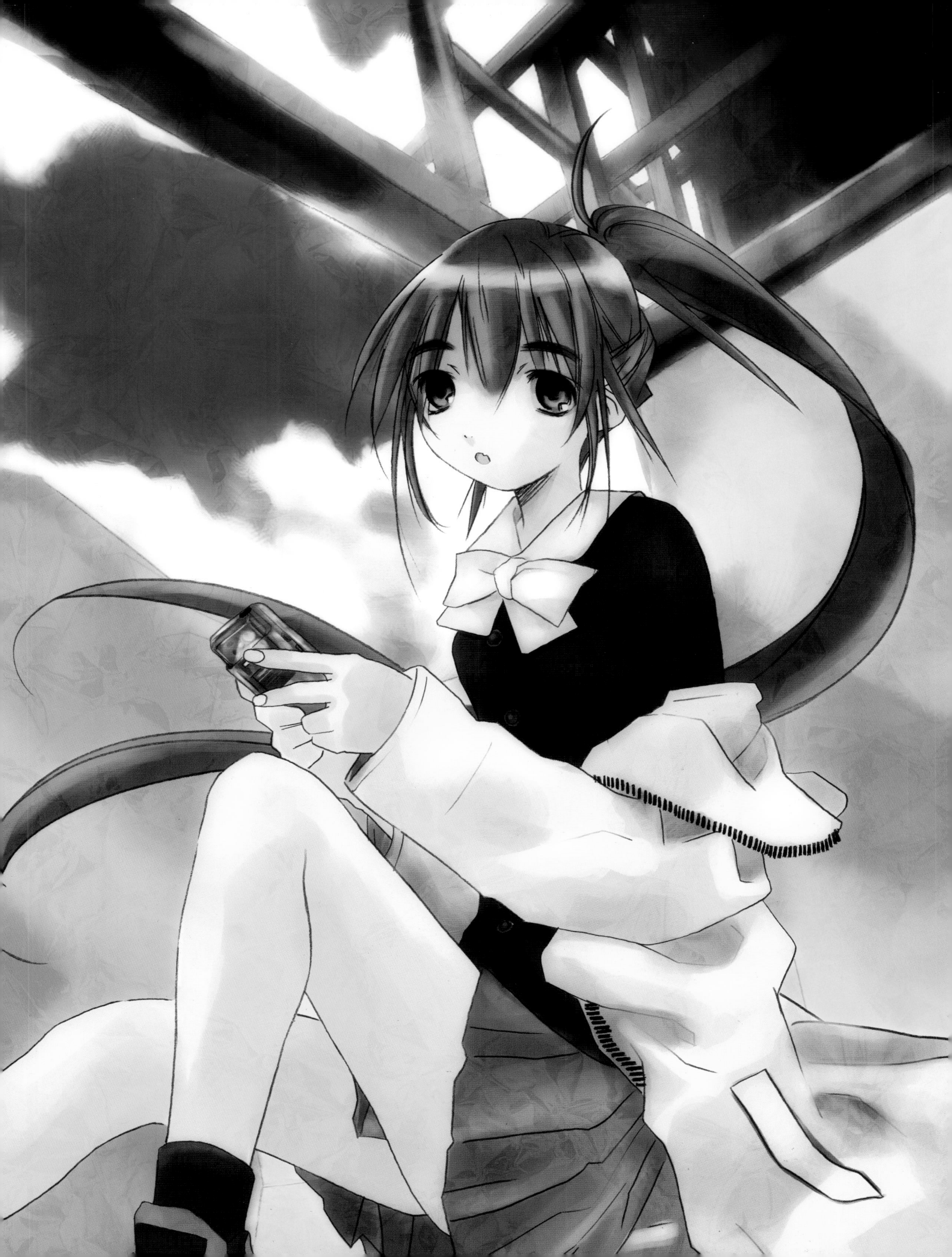

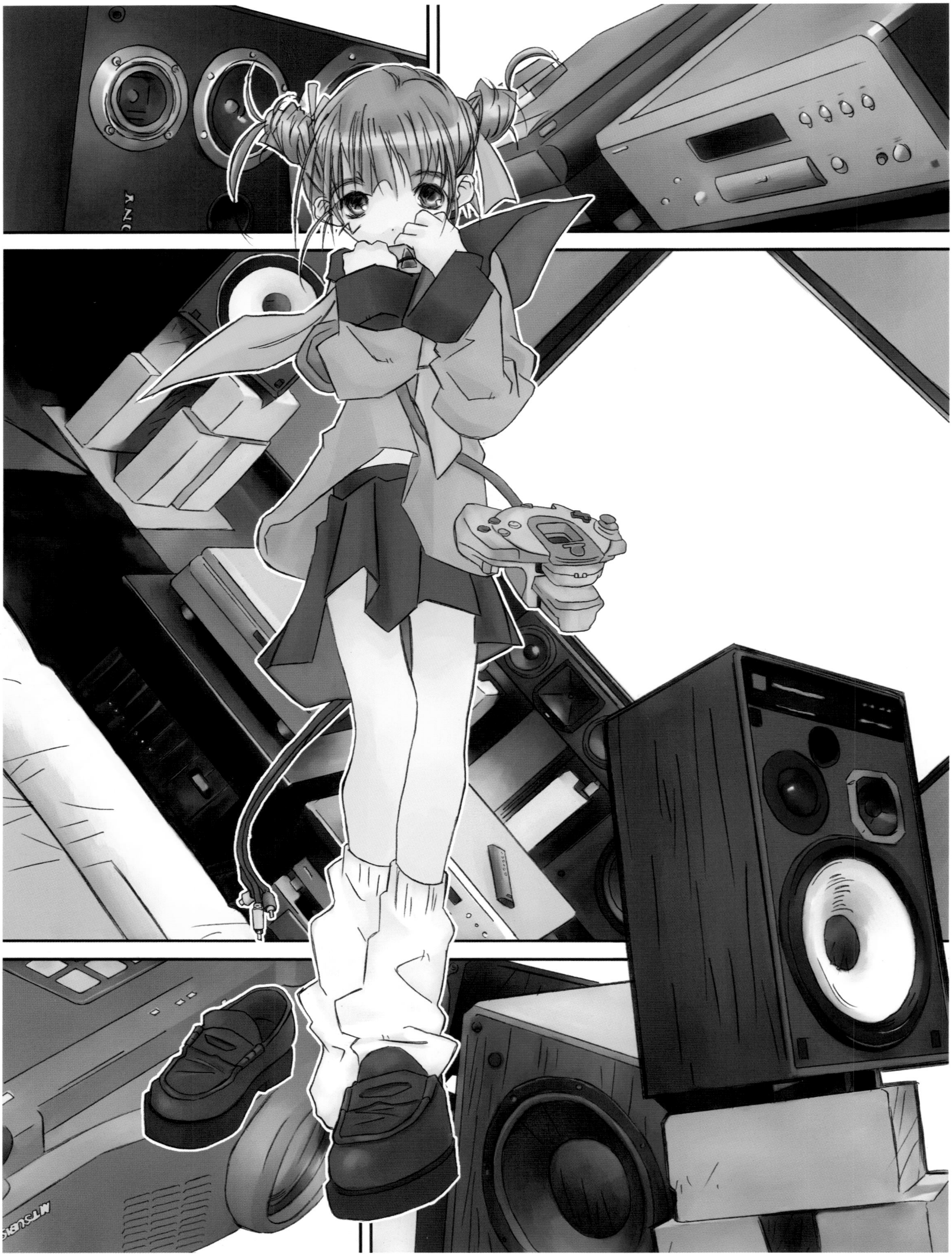

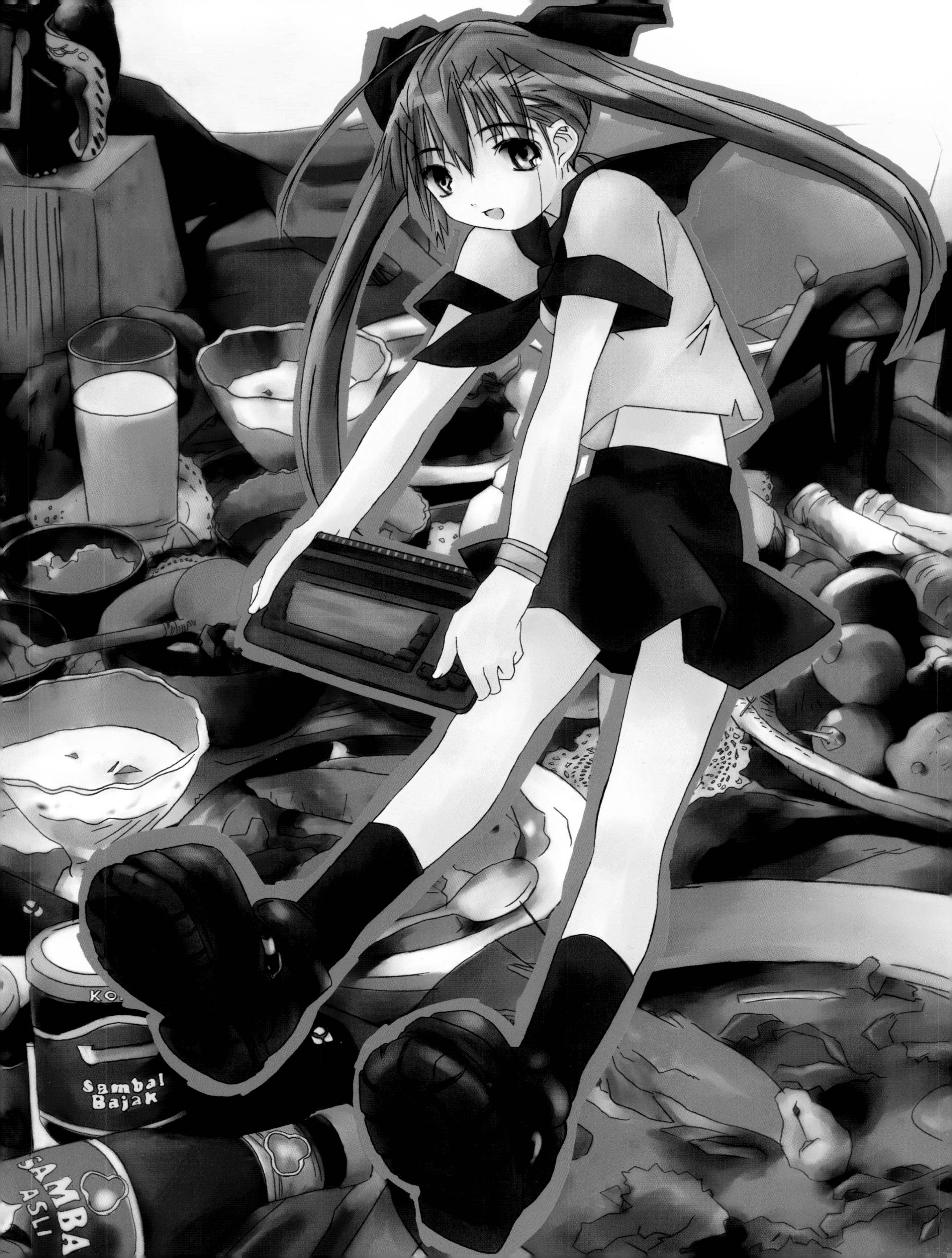
Sambal
Bajak
SAMBA
ASLI

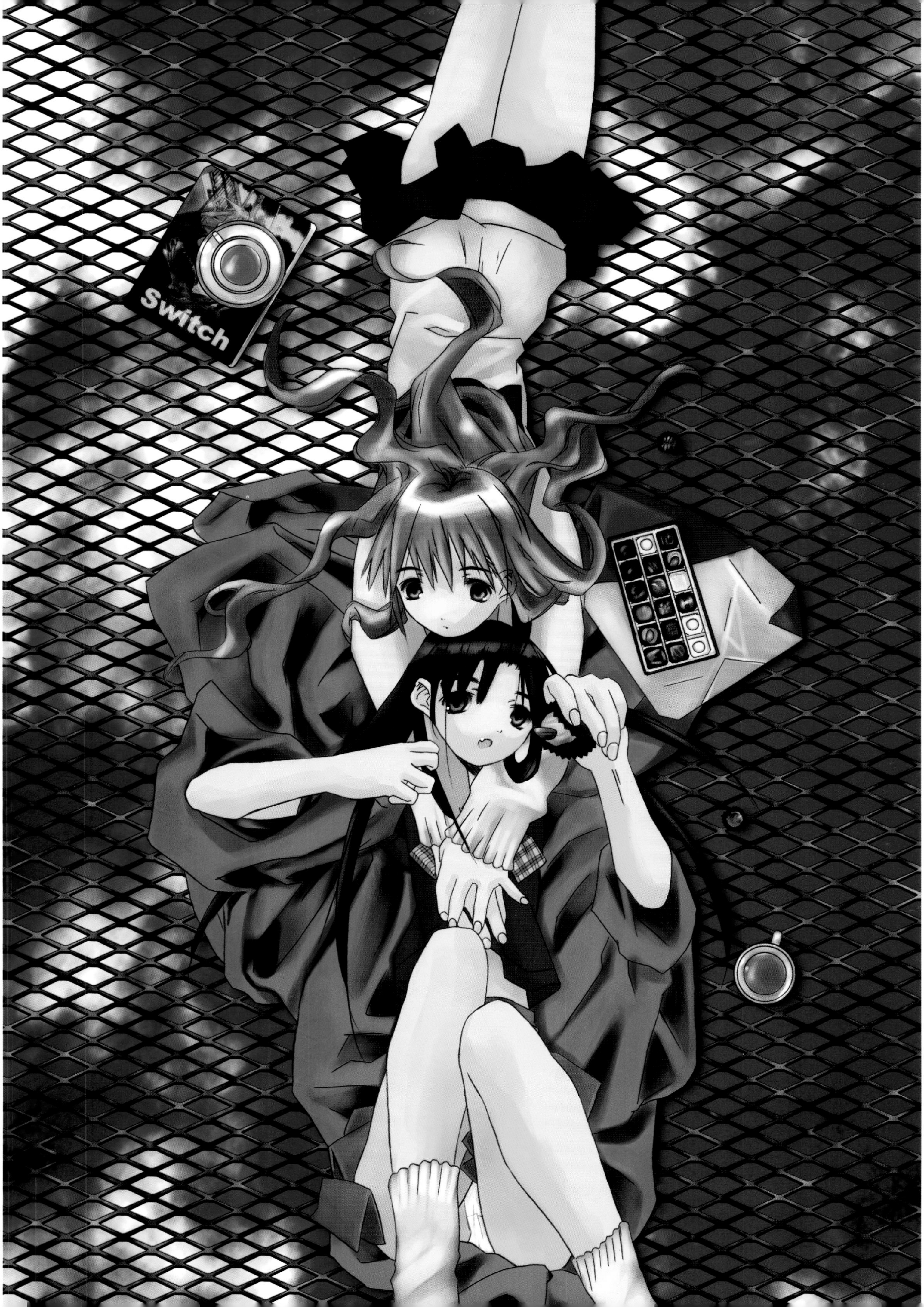
Switch

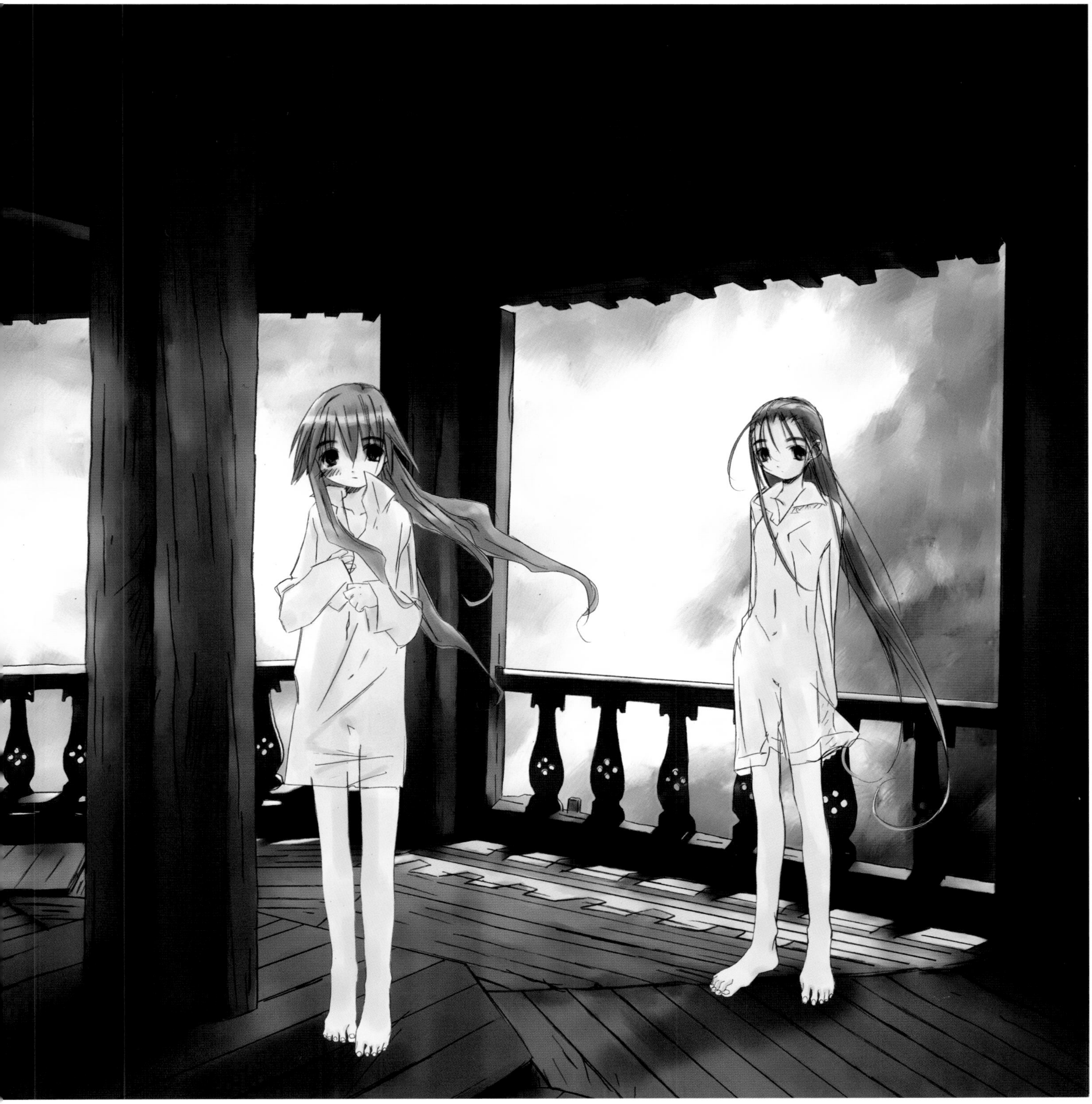

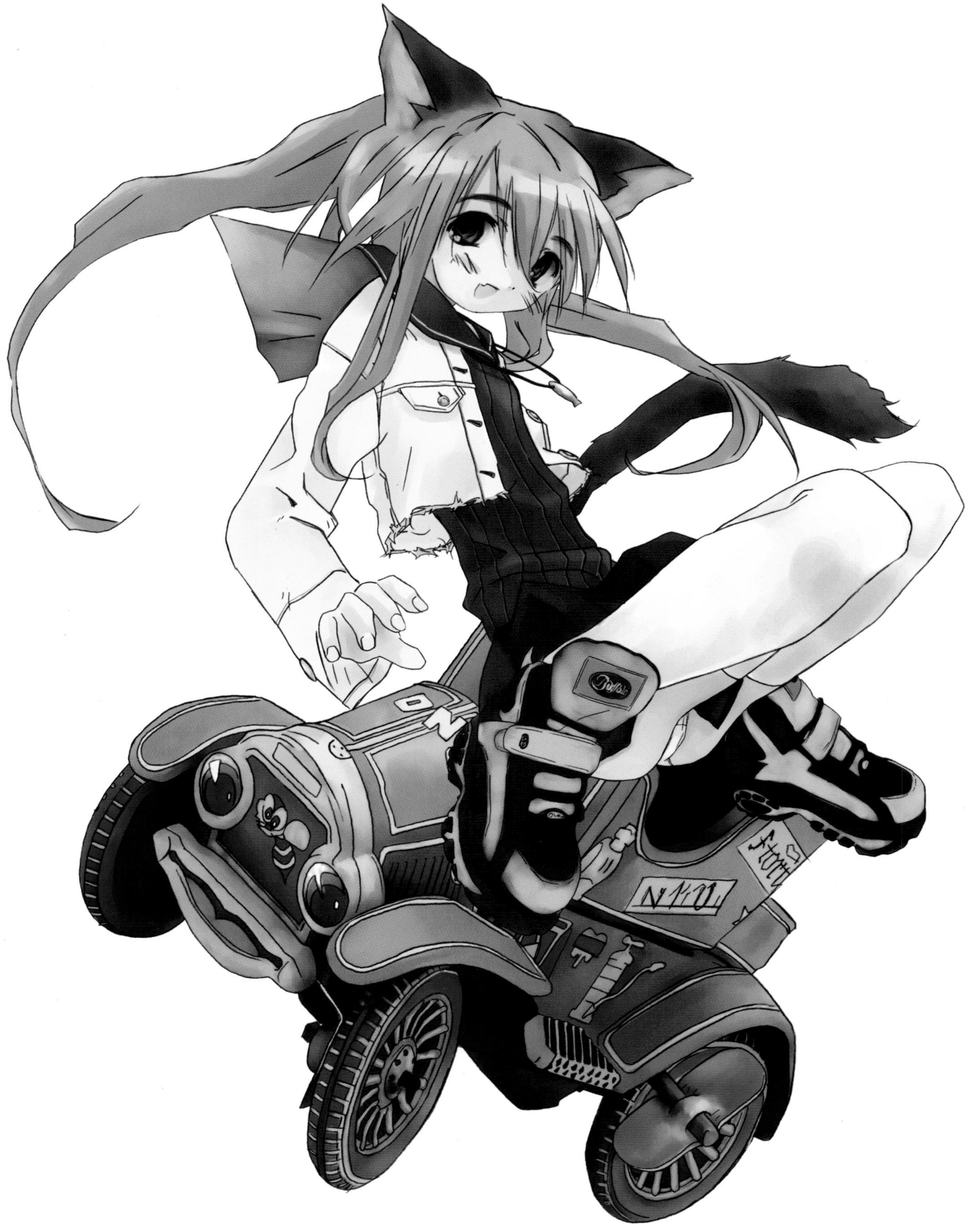

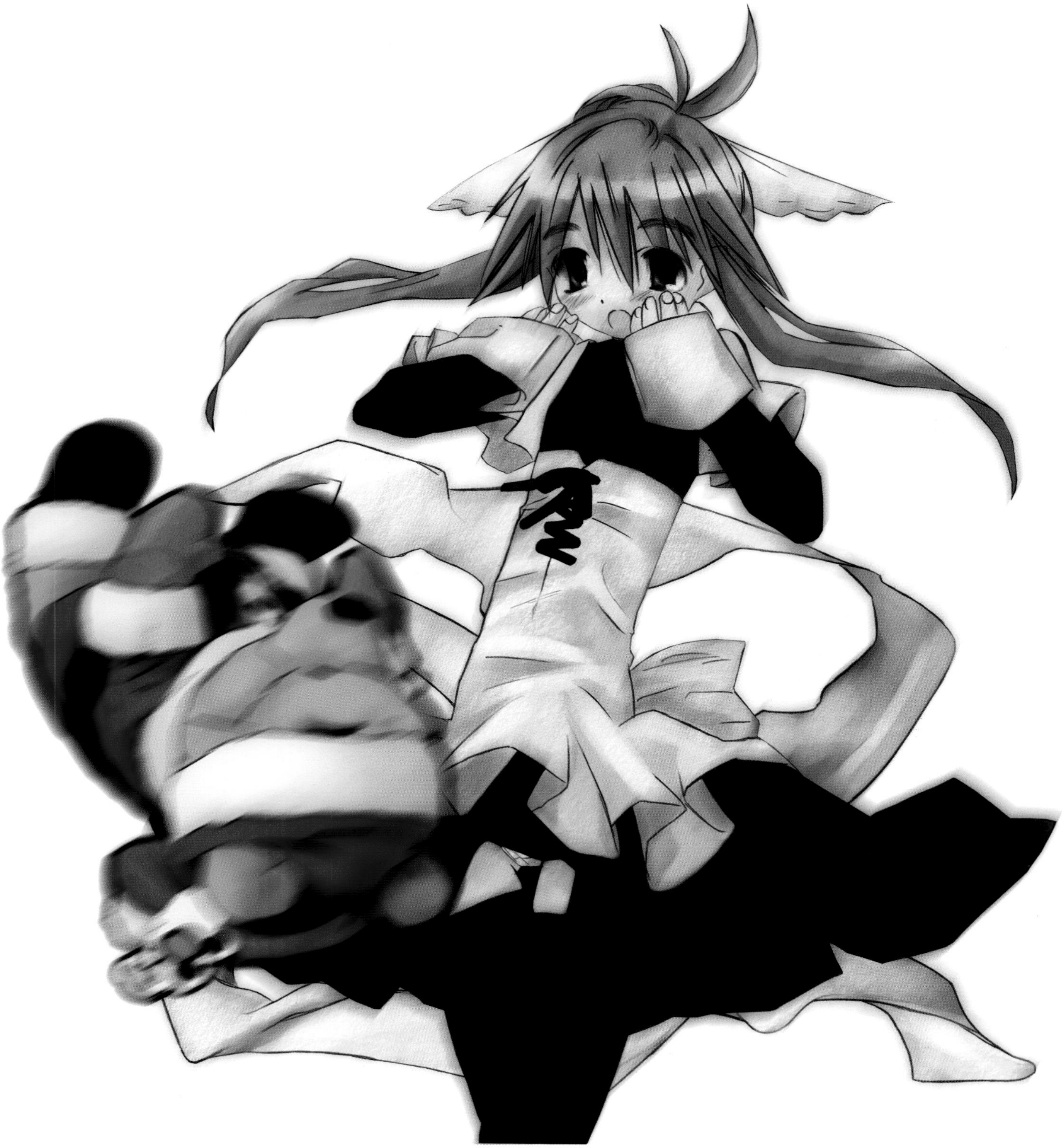

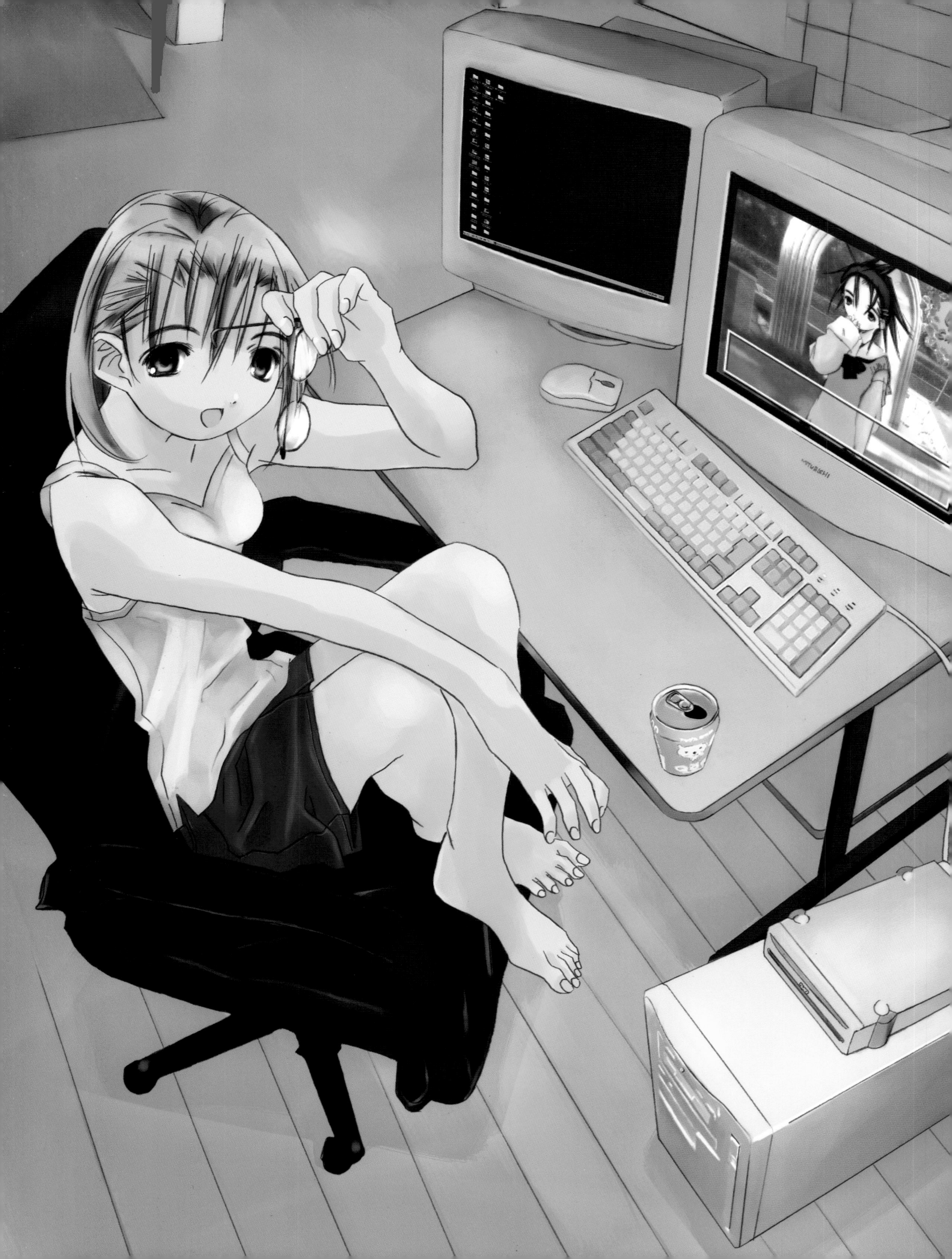

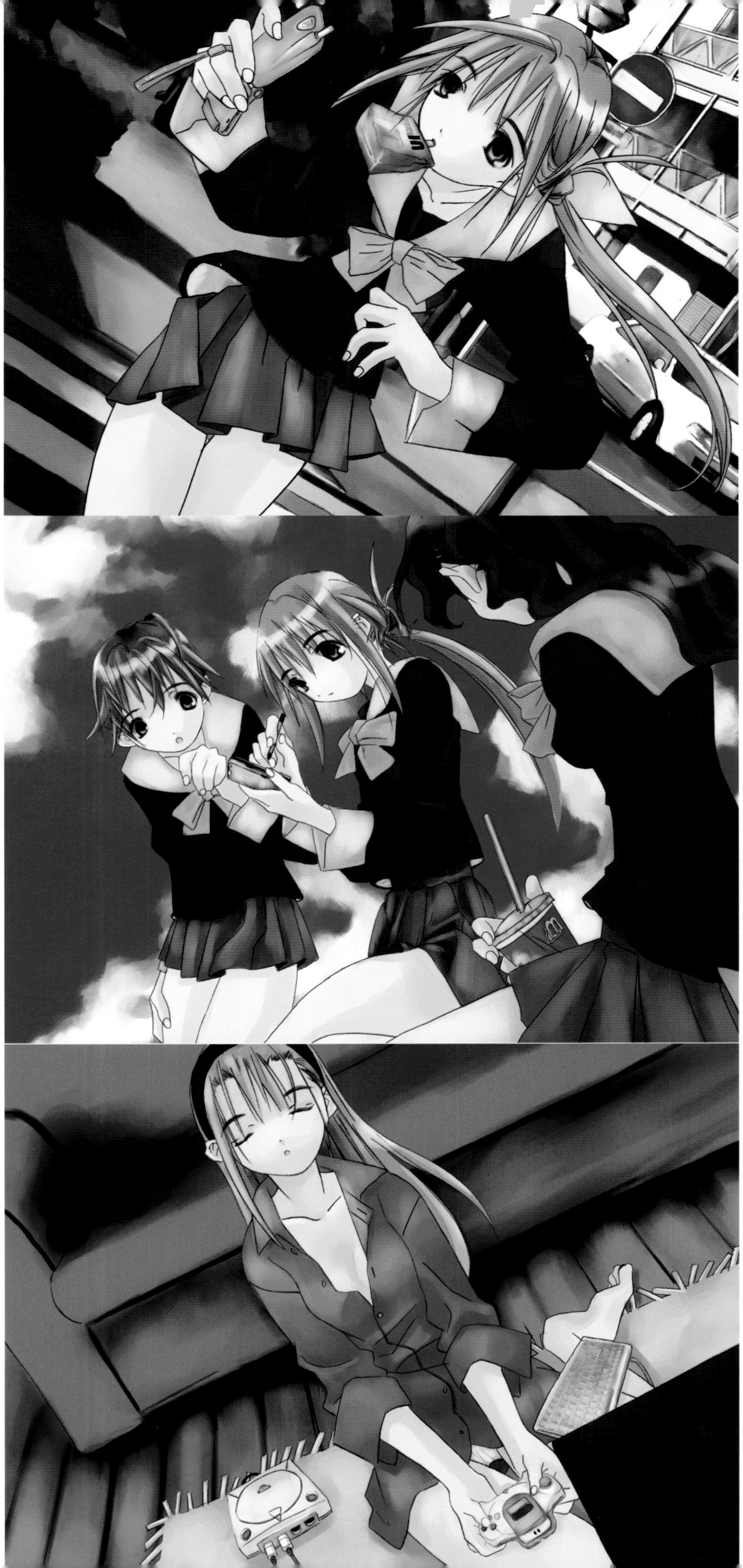

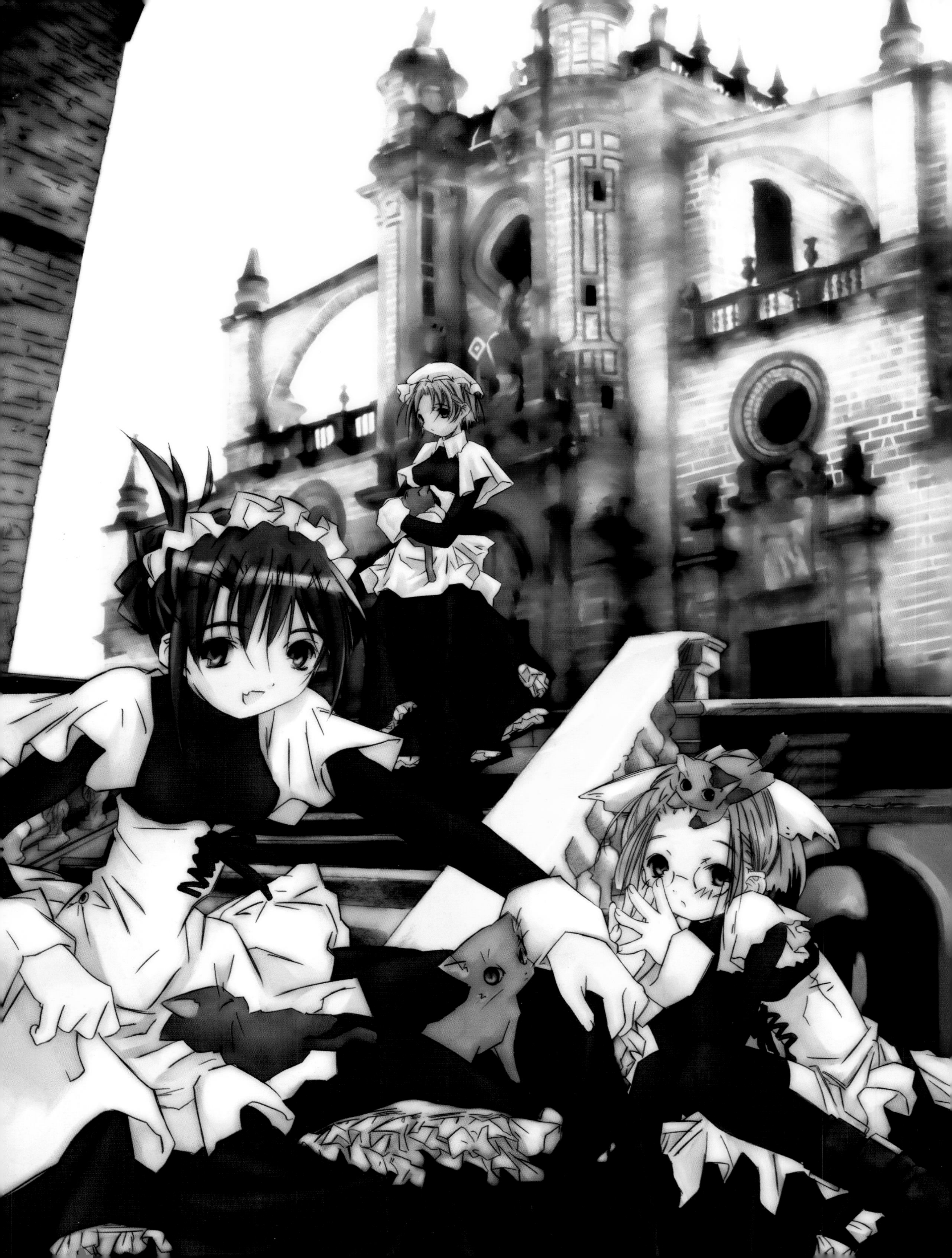

The Artist's Sketchbook

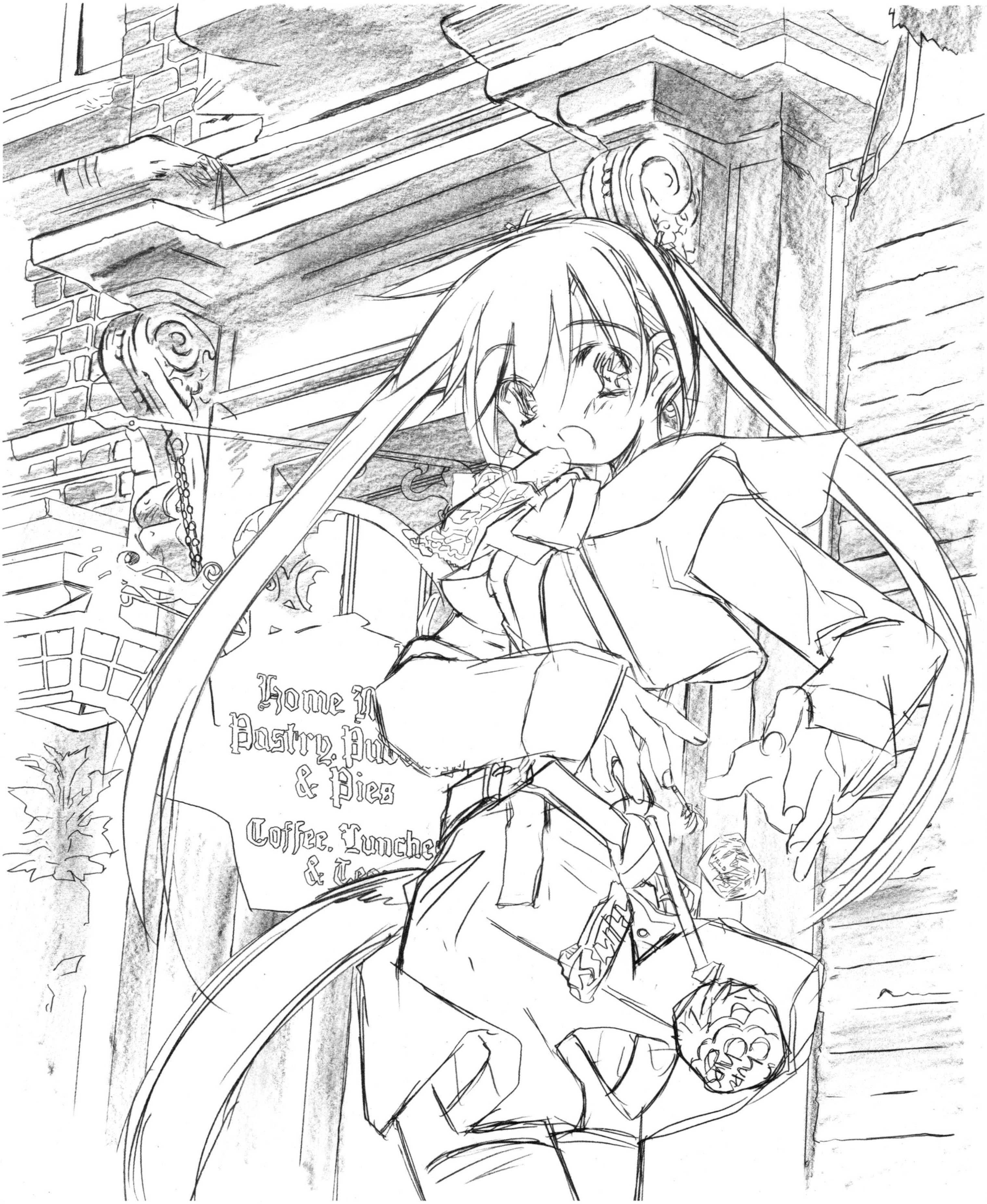
& Pies

This is a girl riding a motorbike, but unfortunately I didn't draw the rest of the bike. ▶

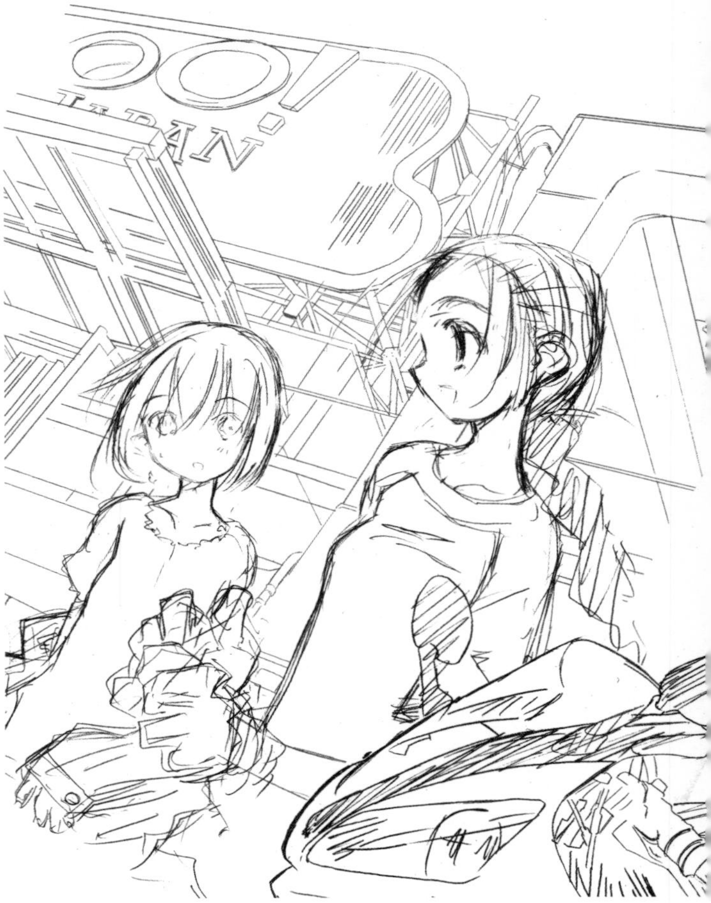

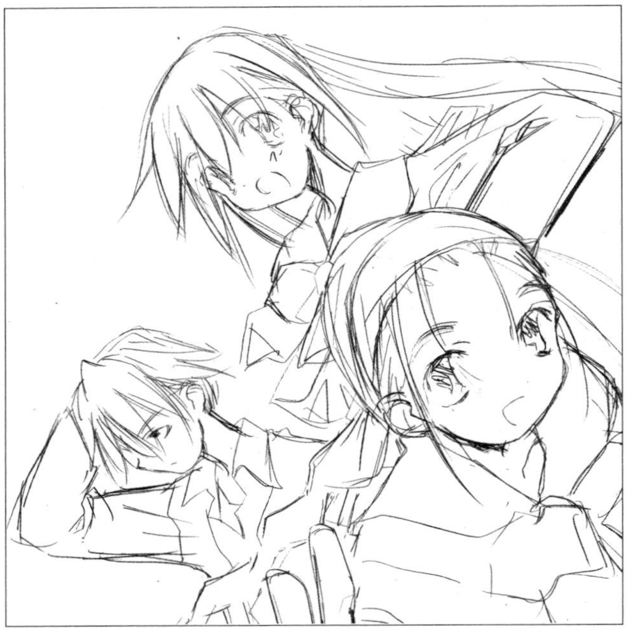

▲ I wanted to draw more illustrations with guys in them, but oh well.

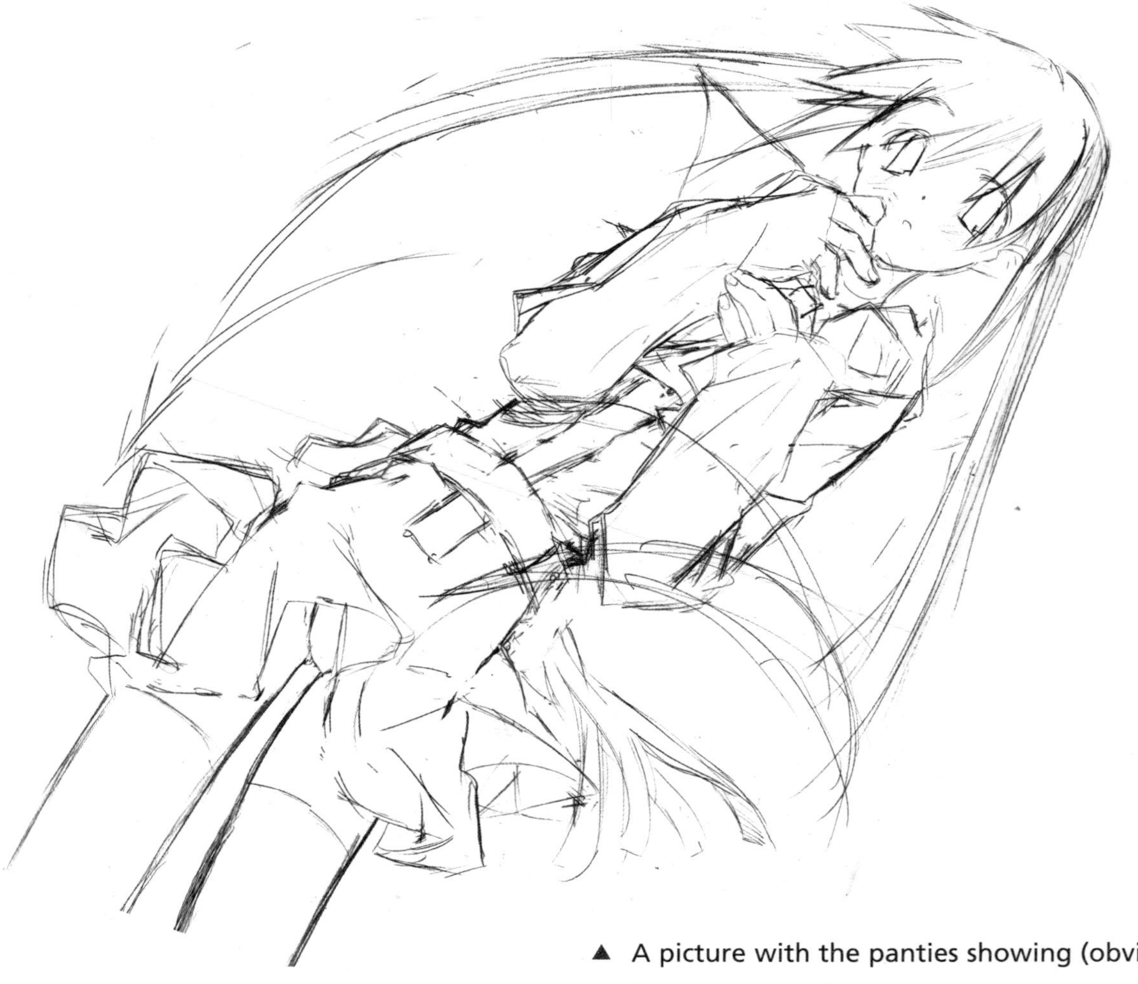

▲ A picture with the panties showing (obviously).

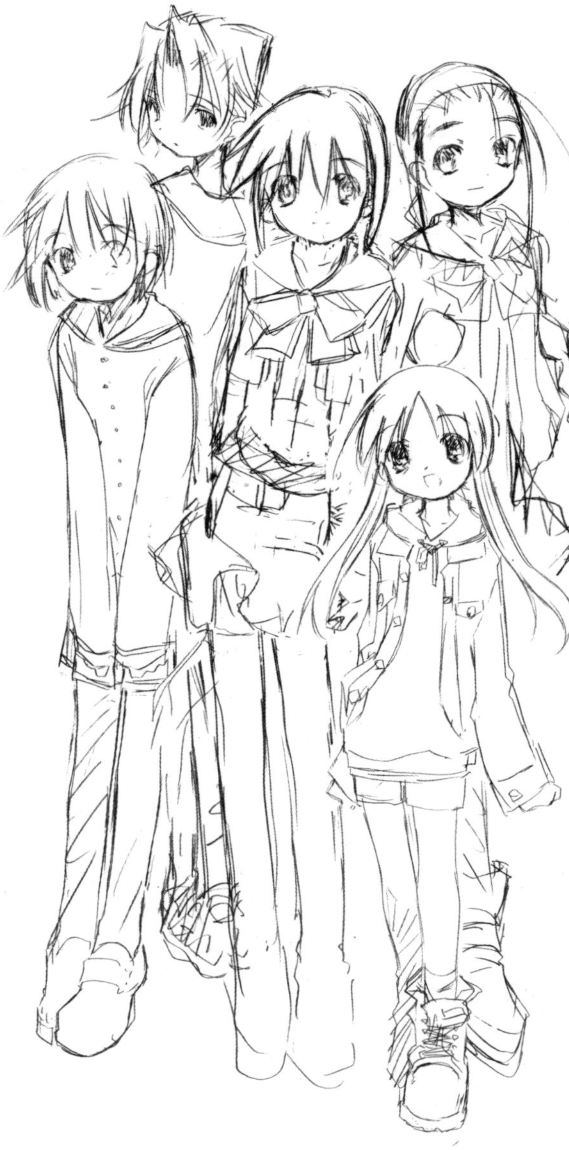

◀ Group picture (there sure are a lot of girls!). Oops, I forgot the hair extensions for the one in the middle.

▼ Rough sketch never used. It is a bit unclear, but here is my favorite piece of clothing in the universe: the N3-B jacket. I draw it whenever I can.

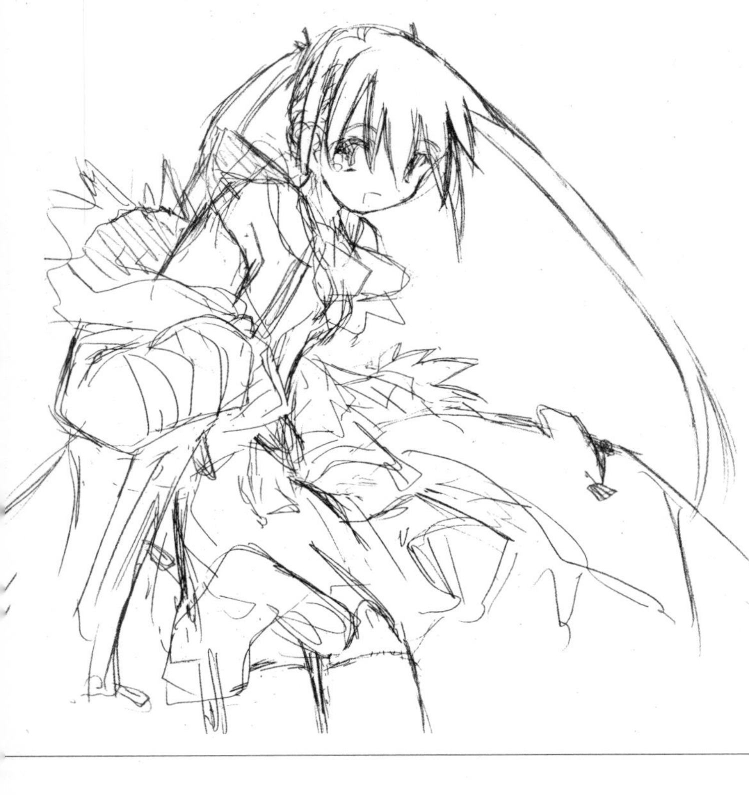

◀ I like this uniform quite a bit. It is mostly black.

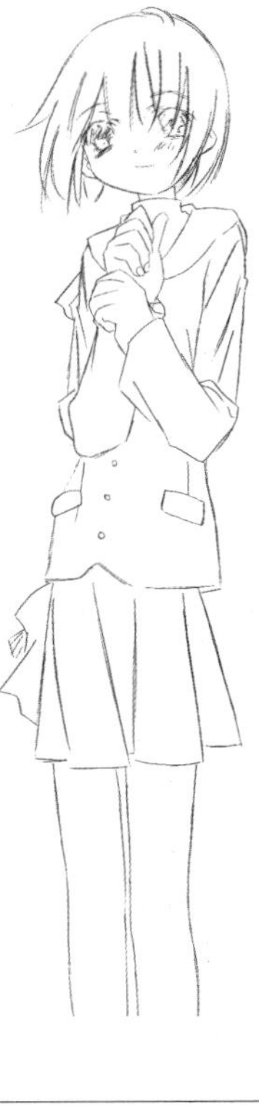

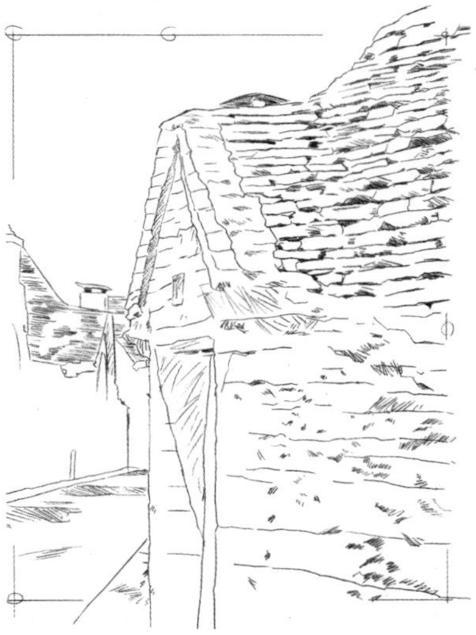

▲ Background line drawing. Where is this place?

Illustration drawn as a cover candidate. ▶ Hmm, I think this one would have been better.

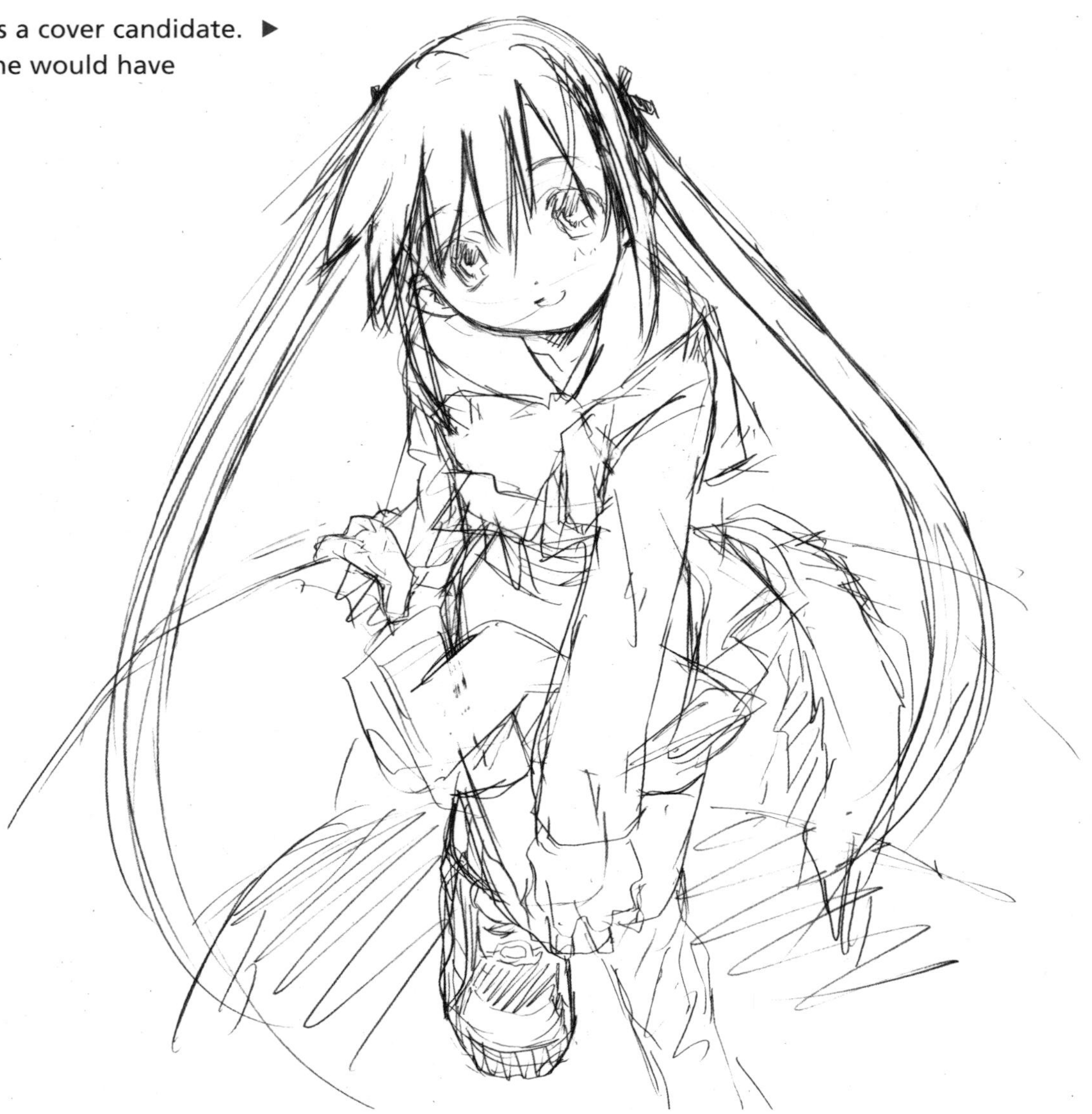

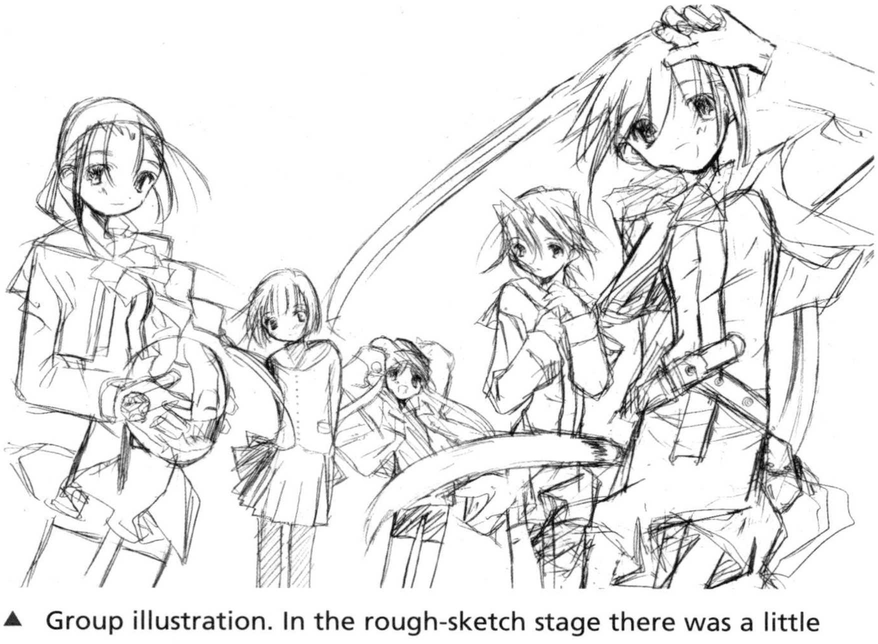

▲ Group illustration. In the rough-sketch stage there was a little girl in the middle but she would have been hidden by the seam, so I left her out. Maybe I should have moved her?

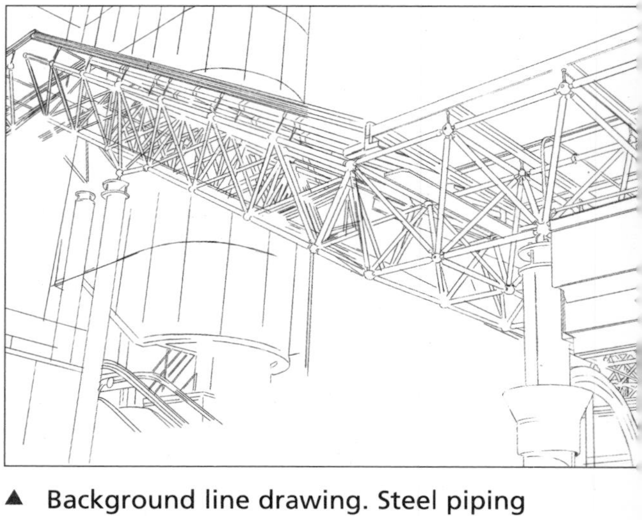

▲ Background line drawing. Steel piping architecture.

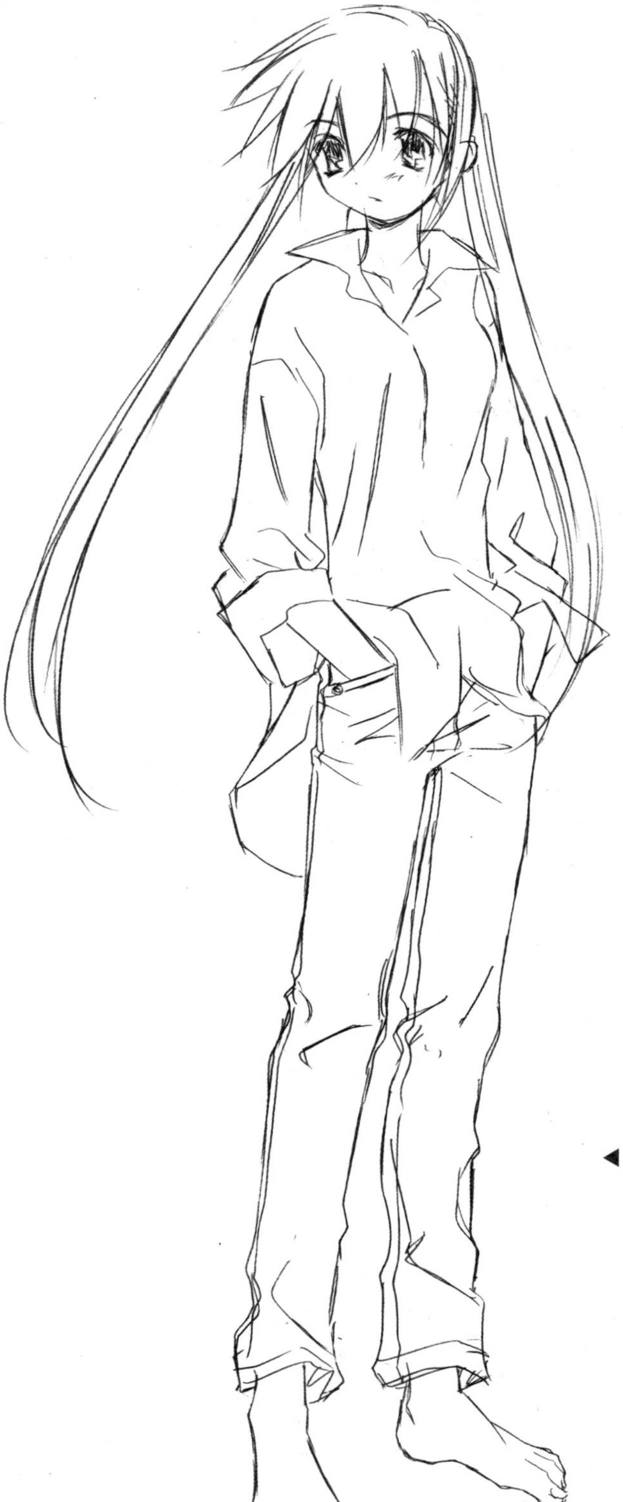

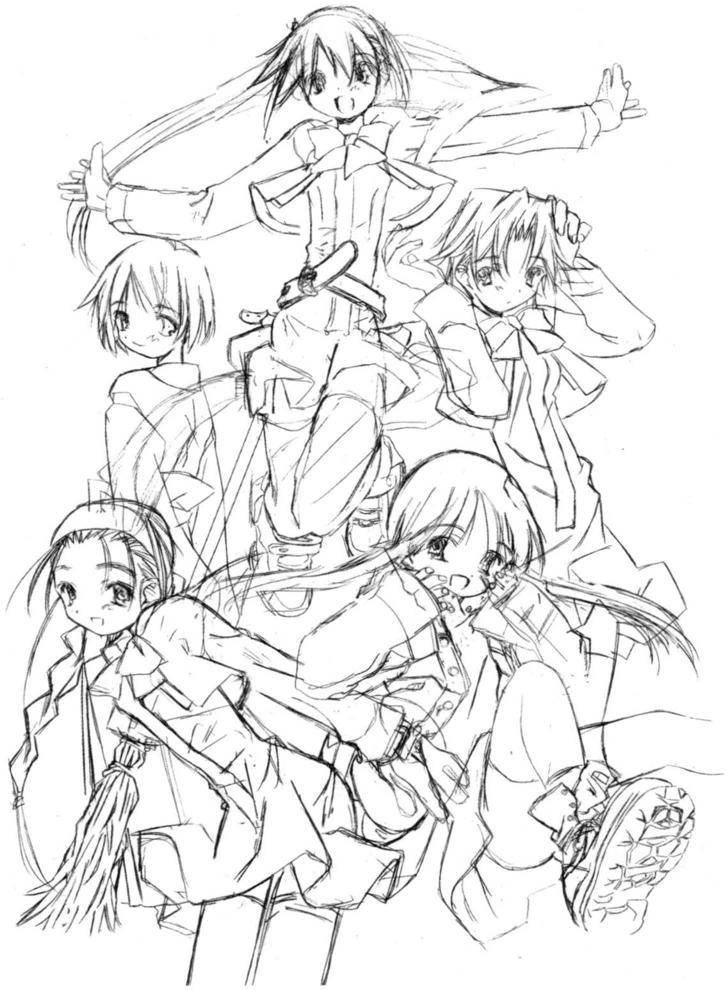

▲ Group illustration. Very typical.

◀ White shirt, jeans and barefoot.
I love super classic.

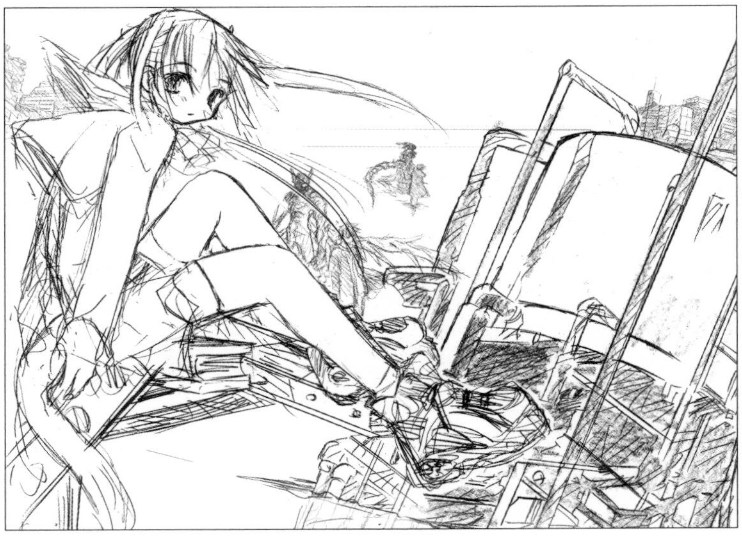

Illustration never used. I drew the shoes in detail even though it was a rough sketch! ▶

■ Mei Nogisaka

Mei is in the first-year of high school. He is able to transform himself into different forms. He has hair as red as oxidized blood. Mei's father is a scientist, who re-created him. Mei's father was murdered. He has a younger twin brother, Go. Mei likes to wear baseball jerseys. His major worry is that every time he transforms, he always tears his jerseys.

■ Tsugumi Aso

Tsugumi is in the 4th grade of elementary school. Her parents were researchers at the laboratory where Mei's father worked. Tsugumi's parents were involved in Mei and Go's first transformation and a fight between the two, and died. Tsugumi then ran away with Mei after the fight with Go, and the two are living together in an apartment in Tokyo somewhere. In the beginning, Tsugumi wears Mei's clothes, since she didn't have many of her own, but now she has grown to like his clothes and wears them whenever she likes. Her character is the kid sister. Her clothes are baggy and are too big for her.

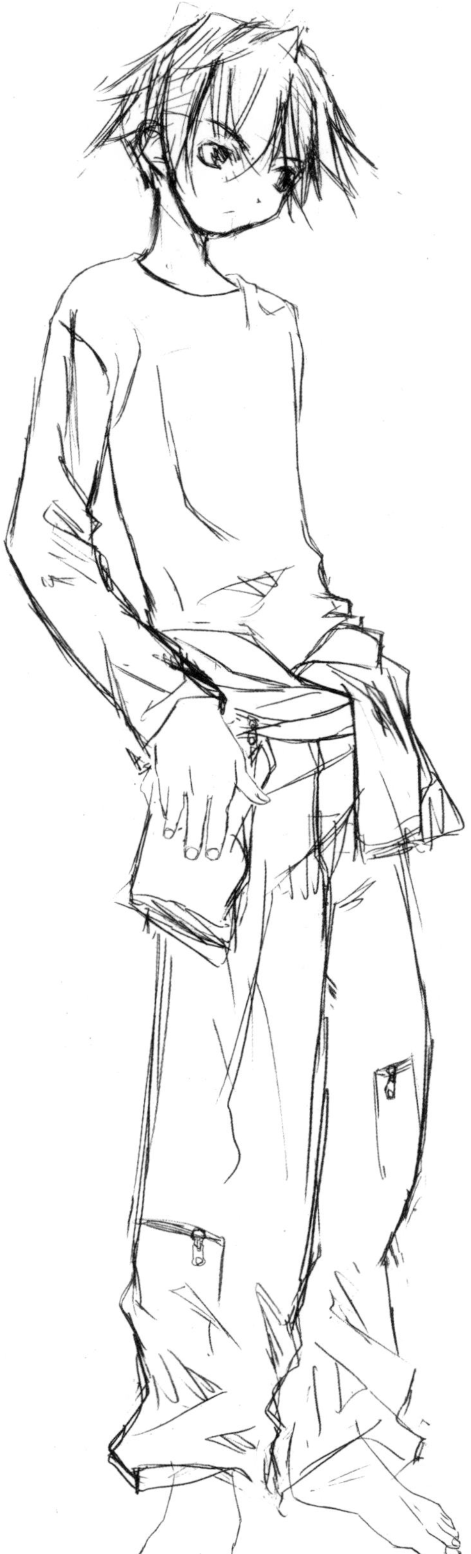

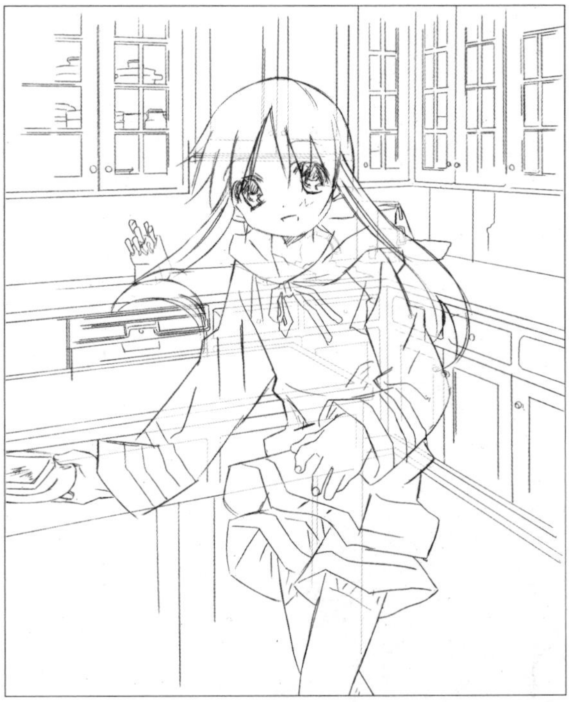

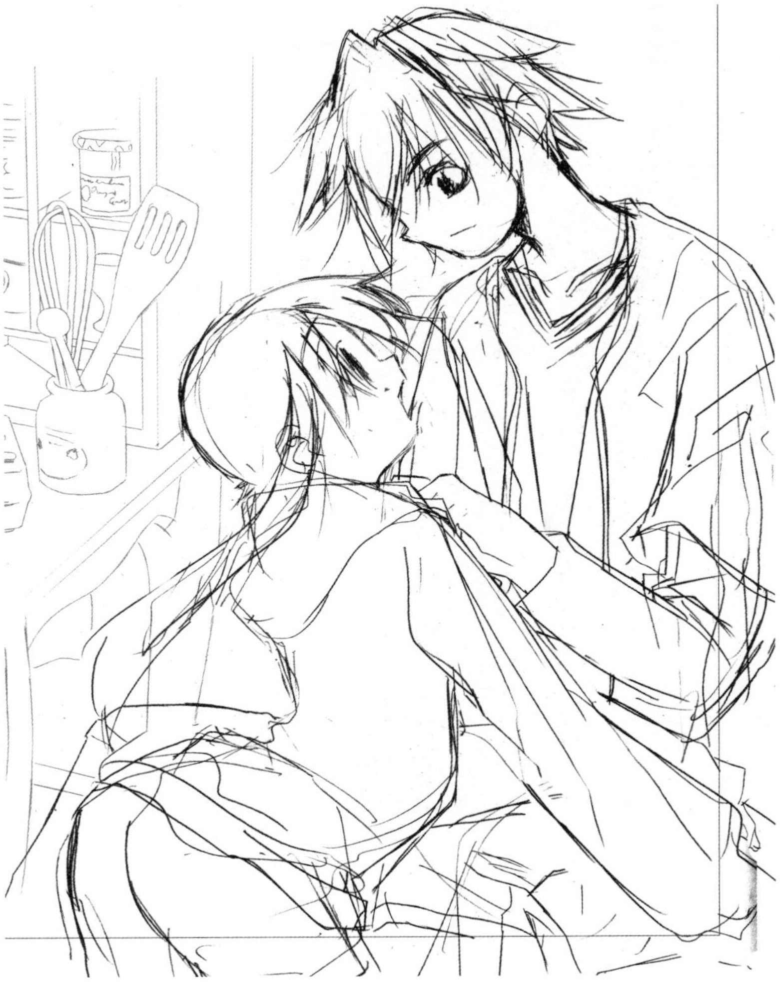

Oriha Hiiragi

Oriha is in the first-year of high school. She wears a hip-bag and fur accessories (fur tail), is quite short (148 cm = 4.8 ft.) and her favorite shoes are buffalo sneakers, though they are the only ones she picks out. Oriha is actually shorter than junior high school student, Kaya, another girl character.

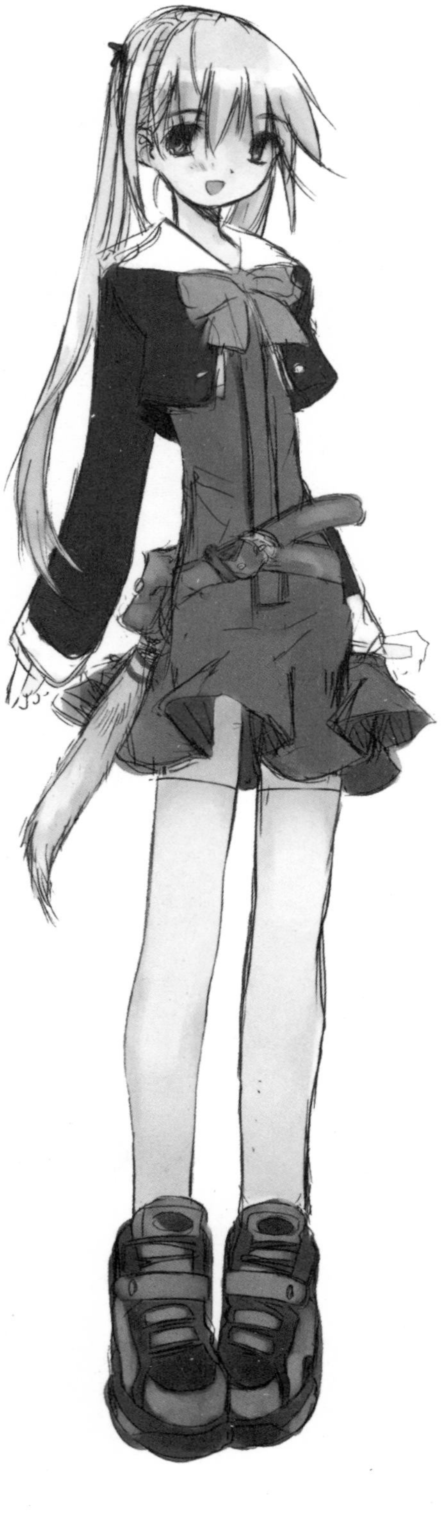

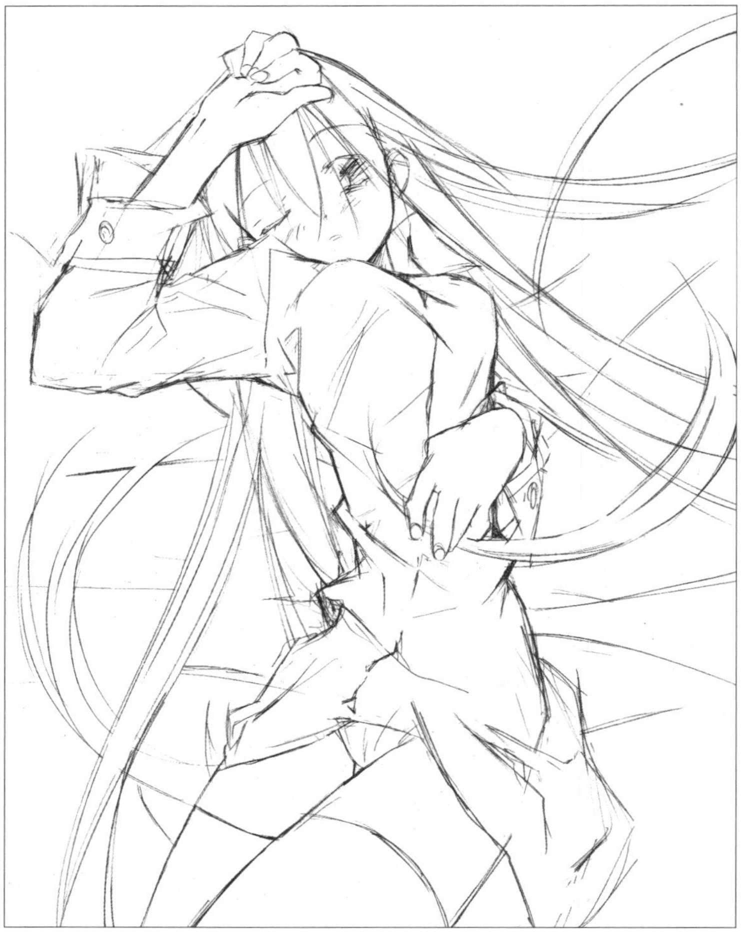

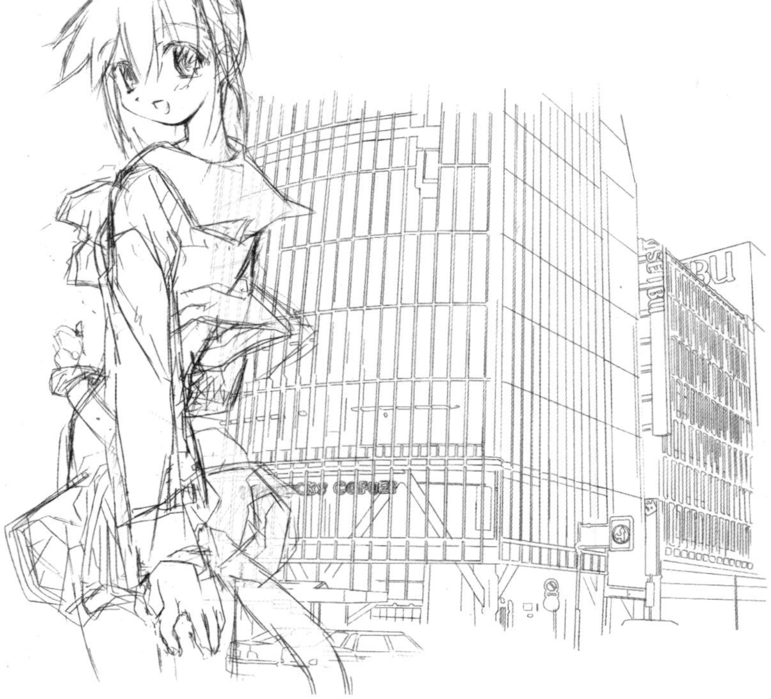

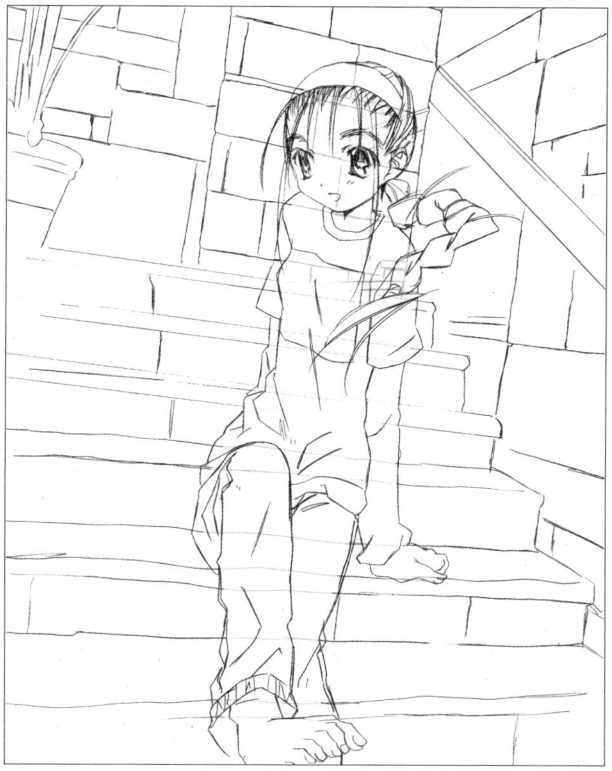

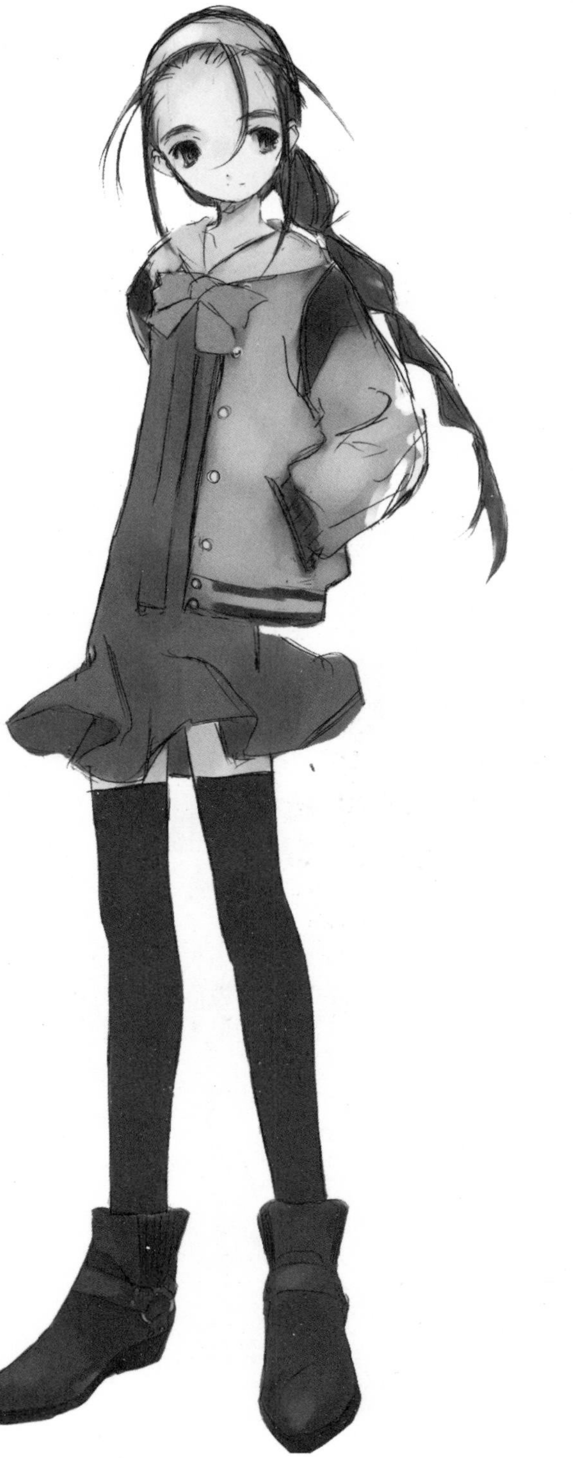

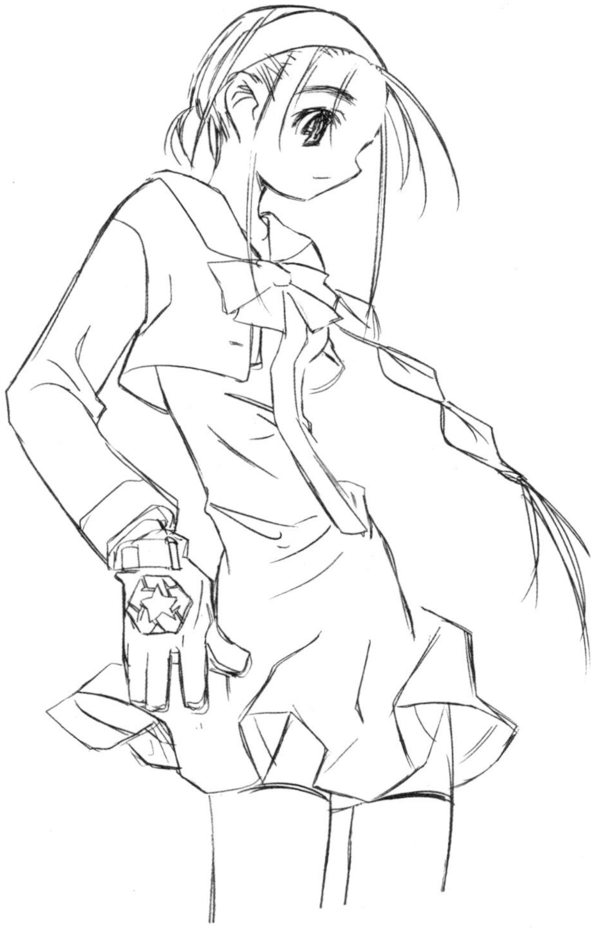

■ Akane Hashimoto

Akane is a girl character. She rides a motorcycle. She tricks everyone into believing that she dropped the engine size of her 1000cc YZF motorcycle, but is really registered to only ride a 400 cc. Akane wears thin, pointed-toe boots for more ease when working the gear while driving her motor bike She loves wearing stadium jumpers. Akane is crazy about films with special effects.

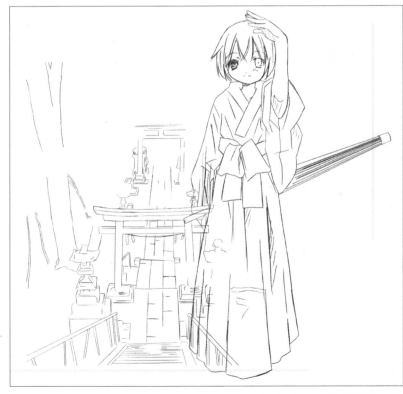

■ Kaya Kunami

She is a junior high school student. She is the daughter of a Shinto Shrine that is closed off to the world. She has very strong telepathy power. Though most of her family is telepathic, she has exceptionally strong ability, and was brought up being rejected because of it. Her left and right pupils are black and gold. Although she has been teased and ridiculed all her life, she is miraculously an amiable daughter.

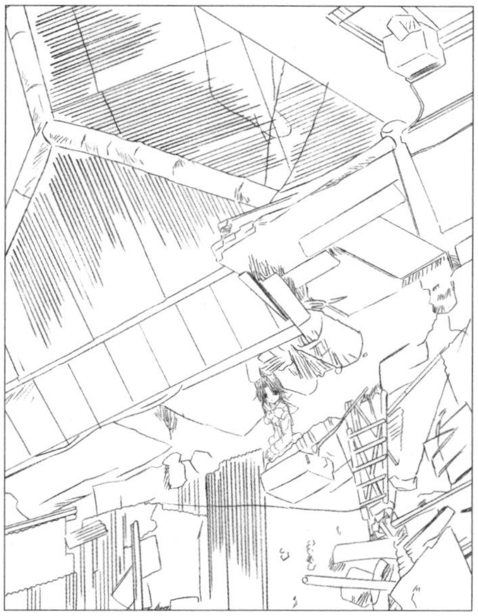

■ Sakiko Fujima

She is in the third grade of high school. She is a beautiful girl with black eyes, but is very inattentive in nature. As for beauty and ugliness, she is not concerned with other people's looks, or her own. When she notices that hair has become too long, she goes ahead and cuts it herself, making it look very untamed and messy. She is in the swimming club. Her hobby is growing plants. As her house is next door to Nao's, they are childhood friends. Nao will always be like Sakiko's kid brother.

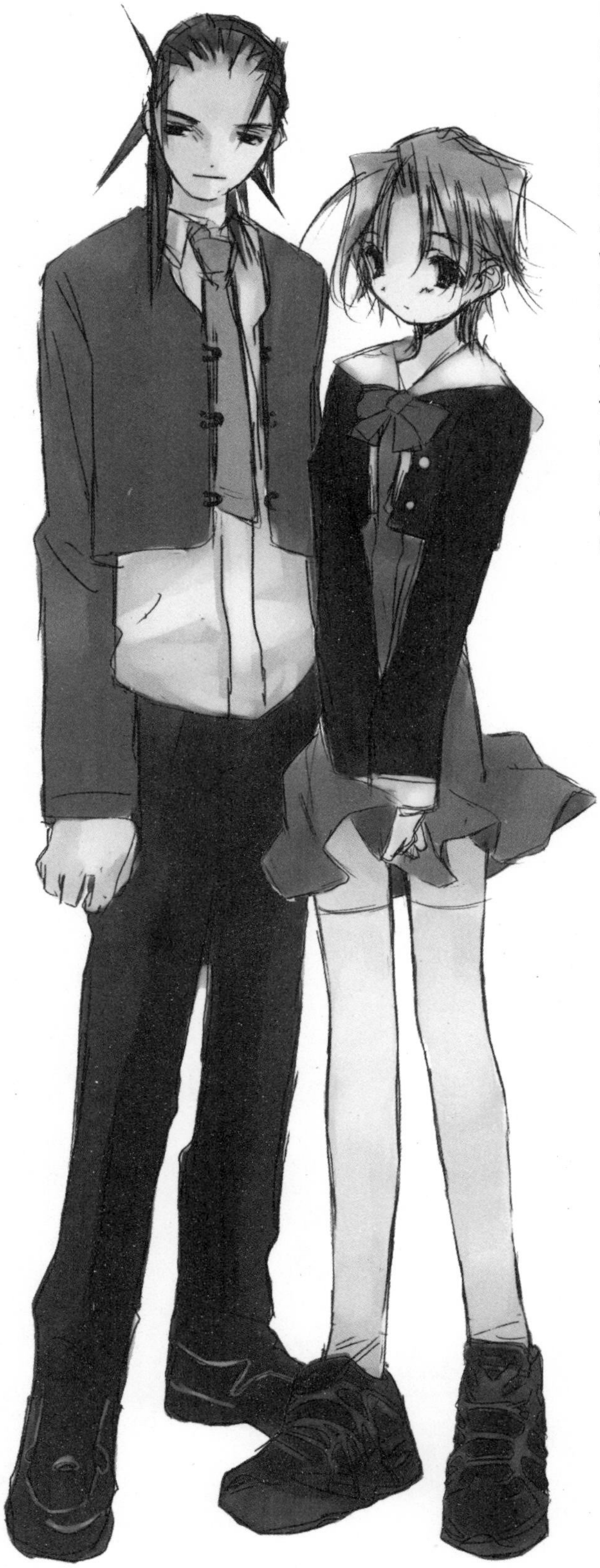

■ Nao Shoji

Nao is in the first grade of high school. He is the most popular and coolest in his school. He can't help but adore Sakiko. Nao has a one-track way of thinking with a very pure heart. Since he is 2 years older than Sakiko, Nao should confess his love before he graduates from school. Under his calm looking face lies impatient, good-looking and comical boy, keeping his surging impatience inside of himself.

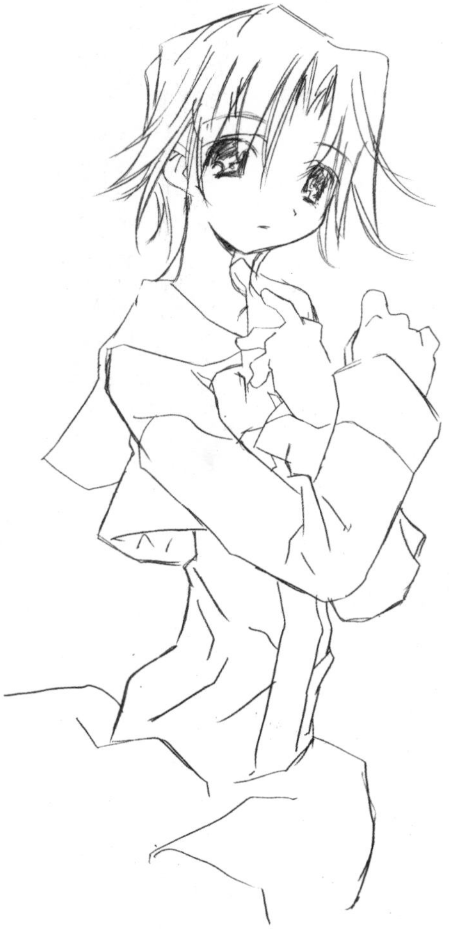

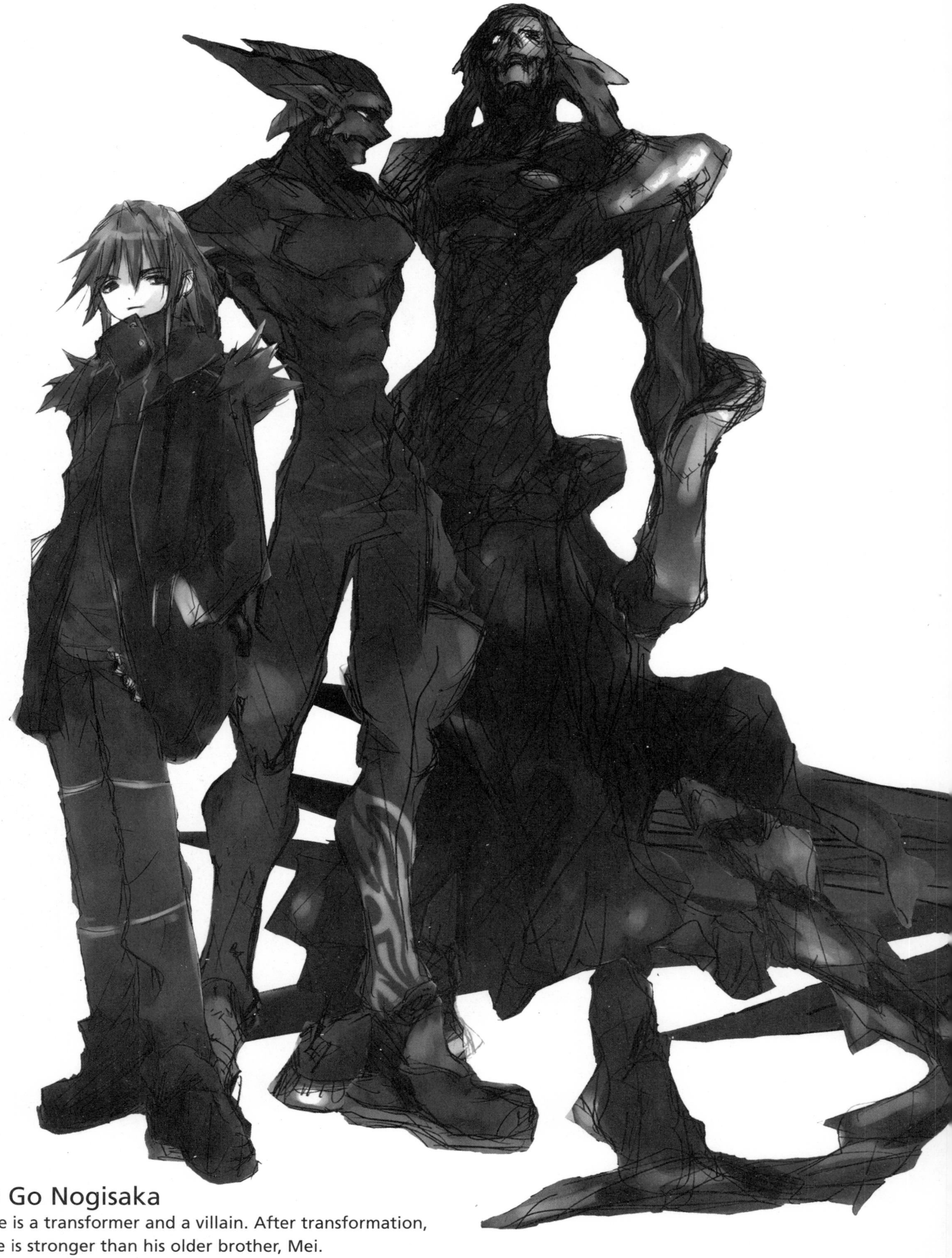

■ Go Nogisaka

He is a transformer and a villain. After transformation, he is stronger than his older brother, Mei.

As for the concept of this collection of illustrations, I first wanted to make a creation enabling to imagine the general outline of the story with Academy transformation-like illustrations. However, I decided to put in illustrations from the game "Renaissance", in which I was in charge of the visuals, as well as some magazine illustrations. Therefore, this collection has unfortunately become something more of bits and pieces of works. As a result, this book does not include transformation characters related to the characters on page 76 and 77. I hope that this whole thing will take some sort of proper shape with another book in the future.

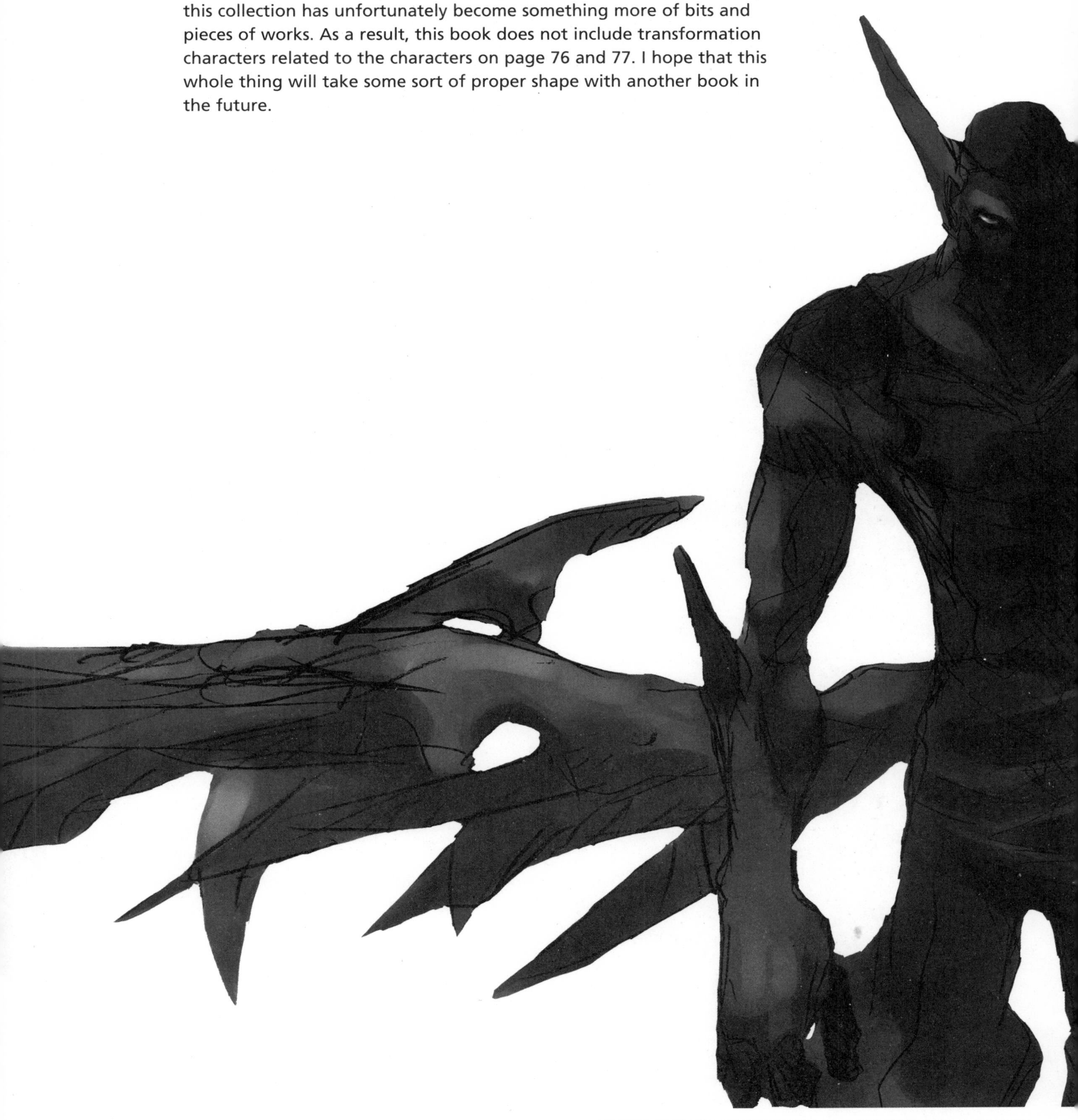

Comments by the Artist

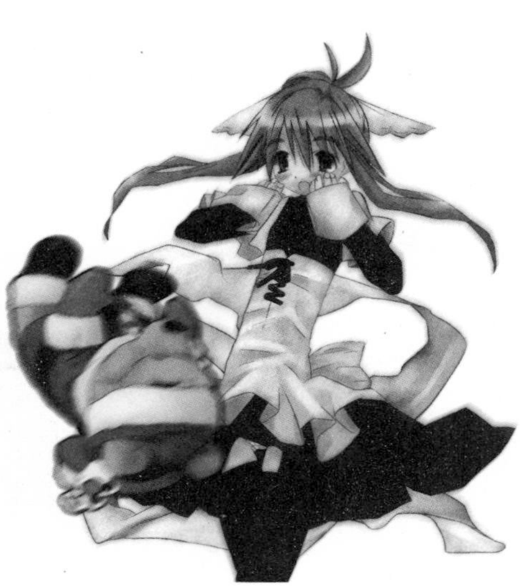

This is an illustration of an original maid uniform and a stuffed animal (The skirt is short enough to take a glimpse of her panties). I prefer the standard black and white color scheme.

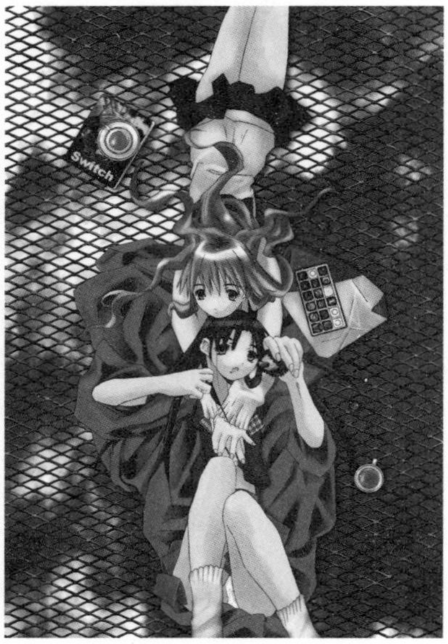
Switch

This is an illustration that I drew for a telephone card. However, the size of the two characters was small for the actual intended purpose of the card, and because I made a mistake in the telephone card's construction, I was pleased that the illustrations were printed larger this time. I put a lot of effort into drawing the chocolates, for example.

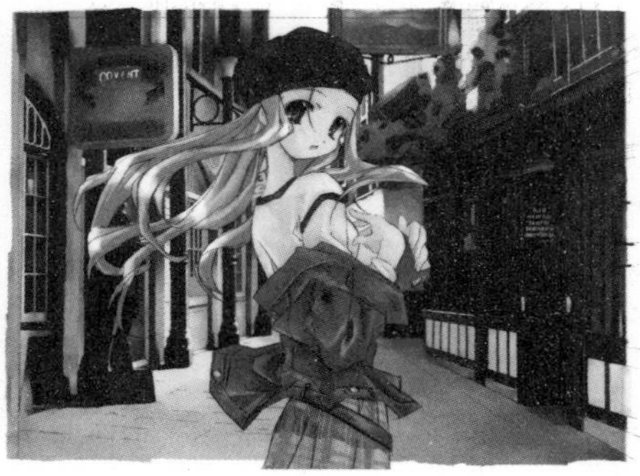

I like the black beret in this illustration. I think that the coloring of the background has been done very well.

A lot of time was spent on this drawing overall, and the game screen inside the monitor took a considerable amount of time as well. I enjoy drawing these kinds of illustrations.

The contents of this illustration that make you wish it could be turned into a movie or a video game that could be watched in a home theater. I wish I had a home theater...
Well, it wouldn't be worth it if I couldn't enjoy it with the loud sounds.

Since this was originally a large-sized picture, I drew many different kinds of things that I like drawing, such as maids, cats and western-style backgrounds. I like this drawing very much.

Credits

P. 34   1999 JIN/Scramble HOUSE Computer Game "Renaissance" Package Illustrations
         © JIN/Scramble House, © SAIBUNKAN

P. 35   1999 JIN/Scramble HOUSE Computer Game "Renaissance" Promotional Poster Illustrations
         © JIN/Scramble House, © SAIBUNKAN

P. 37   1999 JIN/Scramble HOUSE Computer Game "Renaissance" Game Event CG Illustrations
         © JIN/Scramble House, © SAIBUNKAN

P. 38   1999 JIN/Scramble HOUSE Computer Game "Renaissance" Package Illustrations
         © JIN/Scramble House, © SAIBUNKAN

P. 39   1999 JIN/Scramble HOUSE Computer Game "Renaissance" Leaflet Illustrations
         © JIN/Scramble House, © SAIBUNKAN

P. 40-41   1999 JIN/Scramble HOUSE Computer Game "Renaissance" Game Utility Illustrations
         © JIN/Scramble House, © SAIBUNKAN

P. 42   1999 JIN/Scramble HOUSE Computer Game "Renaissance" Game Event CG Illustrations
         © JIN/Scramble House, © SAIBUNKAN

P. 47   1999 JIN/Scramble HOUSE Computer Game "Renaissance" Game Event CG Illustrations
         © JIN/Scramble House, © SAIBUNKAN

P. 49   1999 JIN/Scramble HOUSE Computer Game "Renaissance" Leaflet Illustrations (One part)
         © JIN/Scramble House, © SAIBUNKAN

P. 52-55   2001 Media Works "Dengeki Hime" Column Illustration for June to September Issues
         © Media Works

P. 57   2001 K-BOOKS Telephone card Illustrations © 1997-2002 K-BOOKS INC.

P. 62   2001 Media Works "Dengeki Hime" Illustration on front page of June Issue
         © Media Works

P. 63   2001 ENTERBRAIN, INC. "TECH GIAN" Wallpaper Illustration for June Issue
         © ENTERBRAIN, INC.

P. 64   2001 Media Works "Dengeki Hime" Poster Illustration for October Issue
         © Media Works

SPECIAL THANKS TO:
ENTERBRAIN INC.
SAIBUNKAN Publishing Co. Ltd.
Media Works Co. Ltd.

Profile of Renga

Renga
■Place of birth: Tokyo
■http://rengaworks.hekatoncheir.net/
After developing several PC software works at COMPILE, Renga took a position at Cave Co., Ltd. doing general enemy graphics and special effect creation for the AC game (video arcade game), "GWANGE," before becoming a freelancer illustrator.

Renga gained notoriety with the PC game (video game), "Renaissance," came out in 2001. After that he started new projects and is now actively engaged in producing various kinds of media including games and magazines.

■**Main Work**
 AC game, "GWANGE"
 PC game, "Renaissance"